P9-DND-400

TO A COOL GUY:

FROM:

DATE:

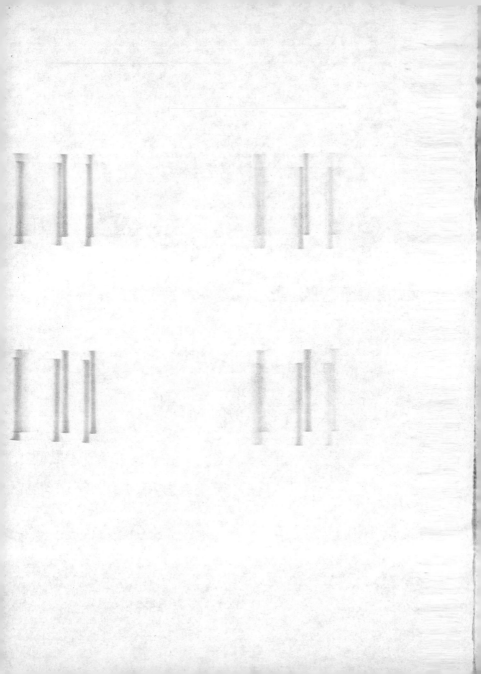

WORDS OF JESUS

for Guys

Carolyn Larsen

Words of Jesus for Guys

Copyright © 2012 by Christian Art Kids,
an imprint of Christian Art Publishers,
PO Box 1599, Vereeniging, 1930, RSA

359 Longview Drive, Bloomingdale, IL 60108, USA

First edition 2012

Designed by Christian Art Kids

Images used under license from Shutterstock.com

Scripture quotations are taken from the *Holy Bible,* New International
Version® NIV®. Copyright © 1973, 1978, 1984, 2011 by International Bible
Society. Used by permission of Zondervan Publishing House.
All rights reserved.

Scripture quotations marked NLT are taken from the *Holy Bible,*
New Living Translation®, second edition. Copyright © 1996, 2004 by
Tyndale House Publishers, Inc., Carol Stream, Illinois 60188.
All rights reserved.

Set in 11 on 14 pt Avenir LT Std by Christian Art Kids

Printed in China

ISBN 978-1-4321-0132-9

13 14 15 16 17 18 19 20 21 22 – 11 10 9 8 7 6 5 4 3 2

DEDICATION

I wish to dedicate this book to my beautiful grandsons,
Jude and Brody. Your zest for life, tender compassion and
boundless energy inspire me every day. I pray that you
will grow closer and closer in your walk with Christ as
you learn to know Him better and better!

DEDICATION

JANUARY

DOING THE RIGHT THING

> "Do to others as you would have them do to you."
> Luke 6:31

Duh ... treat other people the way you want them to treat you. That's not exactly rocket science, is it?

Yeah, Jesus' words are known as the Golden Rule – how to get along with others. But, here's something you might not know – these aren't instructions on how to get along with your friends.

Jesus said this in the middle of instructions on how to treat people you might want to fight with instead, in other words; your enemies.

It's not easy to treat an enemy kindly, but it is the Jesus thing to do.

LIVING IT

Zach thinks it's cool to make fun of Ryan, especially in front of other guys. Some of Ryan's buddies want to catch Zach when he's alone and teach him a lesson!

Ryan won't go along with it though. He knows that two wrongs won't make a right. He says that he will talk to Zach alone and try to get Zach to stop picking on him.

That's the Jesus way of handling this problem.

January 1

WHAT'S REALLY IMPORTANT?

> "What good is it for a man to gain the whole world, and yet lose or forfeit his very self?"
> Luke 9:25

What's the most important thing to you? Is it being a great athlete? Or maybe you want to be the lead singer in a band. Whatever it is, does all your energy and thought go toward that thing?

Jesus has a way of cutting through all the garbage and getting to what's really important, doesn't He? Jesus says the most important thing is taking care of your soul by accepting Him as Savior and obeying His teachings.

Success is living for Jesus, loving Him and loving others.

LIVING IT

Jess wants to be the best baseball pitcher ever. He spends hours throwing baseballs through a hoop hanging in his yard. He runs to get in shape. He studies the motion of his favorite pro pitcher. Everything he does is focused on pitching.

Yeah, he doesn't spend any time reading his Bible, praying or even thinking about God. He doesn't have time! Jess has lost sight of what's really important in life – knowing and serving Jesus!

January 2

LOOK IN A MIRROR, DUDE!

> "Why do you look at the speck of sawdust in your brother's eye and pay no attention to the plank in your own eye?"
>
> Matthew 7:3

Sometimes the things we dislike in other people are the very things we dislike about ourselves but don't want to face.

But we don't get away with that. Jesus said, "Pay attention to your own sins before you criticize someone else."

No doubt, it's easier to pick on someone else for their bad behavior than it is to admit and deal with your own problems ... but that's the coward's way out.

The fact is that everyone sins. Every person makes bad choices. So, deal with your own sins before you start ripping on someone else for theirs.

LIVING IT

Dave has quite a talent. He can find something bad to say about pretty much any person or situation. The weird thing is that he calls out other guys for being critical.

"Jon complains all the time. He finds a little bit of bad in everything," he says.

Well, if Dave takes Jesus' words to heart, he will fix his own problem before criticizing anyone else. Dave needs to admit his own critical spirit. Not easy – but the right thing to do!

January 3

SECRET GIVING!

> "When you give to the needy, do not let your left hand know what your right hand is doing, so that your giving may be in secret."
> Matthew 6:3-4

You can hurt your arm by trying to pat yourself on the back. Weird statement, eh? But, wanting to be noticed for doing things to help others is just wrong.

Sure, it's nice to get a thank you or even a pat on the back, but that should not be the reason you help others. So why should you? Jesus says to love others.

Do your good deeds in secret so no one knows what you did except you and God. God will give you a pat on the back. No worries.

LIVING IT

Zach helps out the neighbor down the street. The man had surgery and can't do his own yard work right now. Zach does it – for free.

He does a lot of nice things for others but no one really knows about it because Zach doesn't talk about it. He doesn't brag about his kindness and he doesn't want anyone else to either. He is a guy of few words but lots of action!

January 4

THE ONLY GOOD NEWS

"For God so loved the world that He gave His one and only Son, that whoever believes in Him shall not perish but have eternal life."

John 3:16

In this Scripture verse, Jesus explains to Nicodemus, a religious leader, how to be saved.

The bottom line is that God loves you so much that He sent His only Son to earth. Jesus wouldn't be treated as a king or anyone special. He would be picked on, persecuted and finally, murdered.

The unbelievable thing is that He knew what was going to happen! God knew, too. But they both agreed to the plan because they love you and wanted to come up with a way for your sins to be forgiven so you could know God personally. Cool, eh?

LIVING IT

Cadon has been to church a bazillion times because his parents make him go pretty much every week. But, he builds puzzles when he should be listening to the sermon. He daydreams during the worship time. He hardly ever listens to the message of how much God loves him or that Jesus died for his sins.

Too bad. He won't really know God until he does hear and believe!

January 5

YAY FOR NUMBER TWO!

> "If anyone wants to be first, he must be the very last, and the servant of all."
>
> Mark 9:35

Promoting yourself will get you nowhere with Jesus. Nope, He makes it very clear that the people most like Him are those who value others, not those who brag about themselves.

Bragging or pushing others down in order to lift yourself up ... not good. Don't brag. Don't be full of pride.

Do stuff for others and help others step into the spotlight. Help others be the best they can be!

LIVING IT

Brandon is pretty impressed with himself. He looks around at the other guys in his class and decides he is smarter, a better athlete, and better looking than any of them!

The other guys get tired of his constant bragging. They don't see any of Jesus in the way he behaves.

Brandon needs to learn that the best way to be Number One in Jesus' eyes is to be last. Humility wins. Pride loses.

> "If your brother sins against you, go and show him his fault, just between the two of you. If he listens to you, you have won your brother over."
>
> Matthew 18:15

Have you ever known any good to come from spouting off to others when you're mad at someone? Oh sure, it makes your friends have to choose sides but then the fight just becomes bigger, not settled.

That's why Jesus said it is better to talk privately with someone you have a problem with. That way a lot of relationships aren't hurt. It is better for the family of God.

LIVING IT

Jon was really ticked with Kevin for the way Kevin treated him in front of a bunch of other guys.

Jon could have badmouthed Kevin to all the other guys. But, he didn't. He handled his anger the way Jesus taught.

He went to Kevin and asked if they could talk. He told Kevin why he was angry. They talked it out and now everything is fine. No one else got involved. Kevin's reputation wasn't hurt. It's all settled.

A DIVIDED HEART

> "Blessed are the pure in heart, for they will see God."
> Matthew 5:8

What does pure in heart mean? Well, something is pure when it doesn't have a lot of stuff added to it – when it is just the original thing.

A pure heart then is focused on loving and serving God. It has nothing else added to it like self-centeredness or pride or any confusion about who is Number One in your life.

LIVING IT

Jason loves to be the center of attention. He cracks jokes and does all kinds of goofy things just so his friends will think he is the coolest guy ever.

However, Jason also claims to know Jesus. Some of his actions and words don't really go together which means that most of the time he has a divided heart – one part wanting to serve God and the other part all about himself. Jason's heart is not pure, not focused.

January

THE BEST DOCTOR

"It is not the healthy who need a doctor, but the sick. I have not come to call the righteous, but sinners."

Mark 2:17

Did you know that Jesus considers sin to be an illness? He let everyone know that He is the doctor. Jesus is the only one who can cure the illness of sin.

That's why He didn't just hang out in the temple with the religious leaders. He made sure He was around people who needed to know Him.

For you, that means it's OK to have friends who don't go to church. You can be a good influence in their lives by telling them about Jesus and living your faith in front of them!

LIVING IT

Jude is a star on the soccer team. His teammates like him because he is as nice as he is good. Jude is a Christian but he isn't pushy about sharing his faith. But, they see his faith in the way he lives, how he plays their games, and how he treats them.

Jude lives his faith in front of those who don't know Jesus!

January 9

WORSHIP AND SERVE GOD ALONE

Jesus knows what it's like to be tempted to do something wrong. It's hard. Satan tempted Jesus by trying to get Him to worship him instead of God.

Satan waited until Jesus was really hungry then offered to turn stones into bread ... if Jesus would worship him.

Jesus had an answer though – "Worship and serve God alone!" That's the best comeback for any temptation – stick with God!

LIVING IT

It matters to Michael what his friends think about him. Yeah, he worships God and cares about God, but not if it gets in the way of his friends thinking he is cool. His friends are so important that you might say he kind of "worships" them.

Maybe this sounds crazy to you, but when what friends think matters more to you than what God thinks then your focus of worship is messed up. Michael needs to get his priorities straight. God first, friends somewhere down the line.

January 10

GIVE UP ON WORRY

"Do not let your hearts be troubled. Trust in God; trust also in Me."
John 14:1

Worry takes over your thoughts. When you're worried about something it's hard to think about anything else. The crazy thing is that usually you worry about something you can't do anything about anyway. What's cool is that Jesus knows that you get stuck in worry ruts and He has an answer. Instead of worrying, trust Him.

Yep, tell Him what you're worried about and let Him handle it. He will. You can trust Him.

LIVING IT

Chris is pretty brave. At least he acts like he is. He acts like nothing scares him. Yeah, real tough guy. But, one thing gets stuck in his mind and he worries about what it means. His mom and dad fight all the time – like major shouting matches. Chris worries that they will split up and he worries about what will happen to him if they do. Chris can't fix this problem, it's too big.

The best thing he can do is tell God about it and ask Him to take care of it. Then trust God to take care of him – no matter what.

January 11

TAKING CARE OF BUSINESS

"When you stand praying, if you hold anything against anyone, forgive him, so that your Father in heaven may forgive you your sins."

Mark 11:25

Grudges are pointless. Holding a grudge against another guy just sucks the life right out of you because it takes all your energy. Besides, Jesus says, "Don't bother praying and asking God for anything if you are holding a grudge against someone."

First things first. Forgive the person you are mad at before asking God for anything. Forgive those who hurt you just as God forgives you for disappointing Him.

LIVING IT

Ryan is strong. Unfortunately most of his strength is seen in how good he is at holding a grudge. Yeah, he's tough about that. He's mad at Kevin and feeds his anger through complaining to friends and daydreaming about how he is going to get even.

Ryan tries to stay connected to God, but something is kind of in the way – his grudge! Ryan needs to just let it go and forgive his friend and if he isn't able to, he can ask God to help him with that.

LIGHT IN THE DARKNESS

> "I am the light of the world. Whoever follows Me will never walk in darkness, but will have the light of life."
>
> John 8:12

Darkness can be a little scary. You can't see what is around you. You can't see where you are going. There are a lot of unknowns in the dark.

But, Jesus calls Himself the Light of the world. So, it makes sense that if you stay close to Him by praying and reading His Word, you will never be in darkness.

Jesus is always with you and His light fills the darkness.

LIVING IT

Brody doesn't like the dark. He gets a little scared when a room is completely dark. His imagination starts going crazy and he thinks he sees things that aren't really there. It's scary. When Brody gets scared he calls for his parents and one of them comes into his room.

His parents remind him that he isn't alone – ever. Jesus is always with him and His light can comfort Brody and help him to not be afraid. Jesus is always with him. Jesus will protect him. Jesus loves him.

January 13

KNOWING HIS VOICE

> "When he has brought out all his own, he goes on ahead of them, and his sheep follow him because they know his voice."
>
> John 10:4

Maybe you don't know a lot about sheep. But, it's like this – have you played on a sports team where you had to be able to pick your coach's voice from all the voices shouting at you? You need to know that one voice.

A sheep needs to know its shepherd's voice. A shepherd leads his flock to food and water. He protects them from wild animals.

Jesus does those things for us. He protects us and cares for us. Learn to recognize the Great Shepherd's voice and listen only to Him.

LIVING IT

Lincoln plays soccer. He listens to his coach calling instructions from the sideline. He pays attention to his coach's voice.

Lincoln listens for Jesus' voice, too. He knows that the Great Shepherd's voice doesn't usually shout. It's that quiet voice in your mind that tells you the right thing to do. Some might call it your conscience. Lincoln wants to recognize the Shepherd's voice and listen to it.

January 14

> "If someone strikes you on one cheek, turn to him the other also. If someone takes your cloak, do not stop him from taking your tunic."
>
> Luke 6:29

When someone hurts you or makes you mad do you want to get even? It's a natural thing to want to hurt him back.

Except, Jesus says, "Don't do that." In fact, He says, "Turn the other cheek. In other words, give him another chance." That's because loving others is very important to Jesus.

So, when you're hurt or mad, don't go for revenge – let Jesus take care of those who hurt you – you just turn the other cheek.

LIVING IT

Donny is a bully. That's the honest truth. He picks on guys who are smaller than him and one of his favorite targets is Charley.

Charley and some of Donny's other victims think about ganging up on him to get even. But then Charley remembers what Jesus taught and decides to not do anything. He thinks he will just try praying for Donny and love him from afar. Someday, though it may not be for a while, someday that love will get through to Donny.

January 15

USEFUL FLAVOR

"You are the salt of the earth. But if the salt loses its saltiness, how can it be made salty again? It is no longer good for anything, except to be thrown out and trampled by men."
Matthew 5:13

Salt has many uses but the most familiar one is as a flavor for food. But, if salt is old and loses its flavor, it is pretty much useless.

Jesus said His followers are like salt. We flavor the world around us by living like Jesus and showing His love and values to others.

But, if we stop living for Jesus, we lose our usefulness and are of no help to His work on this earth.

LIVING IT

Sam's friends know that he goes to church. They know that he reads his Bible and prays, too. Sam tries to obey Jesus.

Sam's friends are careful about the jokes they tell and the words they use and the things they do when he is around. That's how Sam is salt to his friends. He "flavors" their world because he loves and obeys Jesus.

January 16

"I am the resurrection and the life. He who believes in Me will live, even though he dies; and whoever lives and believes in Me will never die."
John 11:25-26

A guy your age probably doesn't think about it much, but the fact is everyone is going to die. Death is something everyone faces.

A basic part of the Christian faith is knowing that God has power over death. God raised Jesus back to life after He was murdered and Jesus promises His children that even after we die, we will live again in heaven with Him forever!

LIVING IT

Chris never thought about death much until one of his dad's friends died. Chris' dad and this friend used to spend a lot of time together and Chris' dad is really sad now.

But, Chris and his dad know Jesus and their friend did, too. So Chris knows that his dad will get to see his friend again someday in heaven, alive together forever. Jesus promised!

THE GREATEST COMMANDMENT

> "Love the Lord your God with all your heart and with all your soul and with all your mind and with all your strength."
>
> Mark 12:30

This wasn't just some idle comment Jesus made. He says this is the greatest of all the commandments. So there's no doubt that it's important.

Read it again. There's no room for anything to be more important to you than God. He says to give Him all your heart, soul, mind and strength.

Obeying and serving Him should be number one in your life.

LIVING IT

Rob loves making other kids laugh. He's a real clown. When he isn't doing something goofy he is playing the guitar. Music is his second love. Rob puts lots of energy, thought and time into entertaining others and learning new songs. He tries to fit in living for God or reading his Bible and even praying around those other things.

Yeah, that's not going to work. God must be Number One! He doesn't share that spot with anything or anyone else. Rob has some choices to make.

LOVING OTHERS

> "The second is this: 'Love your neighbor as yourself.' There is no commandment greater than these."
>
> Mark 12:31

Part two of the commandments Jesus said are the most important is to love your neighbor. This goes with the previous verse because if you love God with all your heart, soul, mind and strength, you can't help but love your neighbor.

"Who is my neighbor?" you might ask. Simple answer – anyone around you.

Loving others means you think about what is best for them before you think about yourself and what you want. This is just about the opposite of what the world says!

LIVING IT

For weeks Kenneth has looked forward to going to a major league baseball game with his buddy Daniel. Kenneth loves baseball but doesn't get to go to many games. But the very day of the game Kenneth's mom got really sick and his dad asked him to skip the game so he could help with his younger brother and sister.

It isn't what Kenneth wants to do – but it's the right thing to do. He stays home with his young brother and sister and helps them not be worried about their mom. Loving others sometimes means loving your own family!

GOD CAN DO ANYTHING!

> "With man this is impossible, but with God all things are possible."
> Matthew 19:26

In the words of a children's song, "There is nothing your God cannot do!" Jesus said this when He was talking about how hard it is for people to get into heaven.

The truth is that if it were left up to humans, it would not be possible to make a way for people to go to heaven. But, God is the Creator of every thing. He can do anything! Since God wanted to make a way for people to go to heaven, He did it.

There is nothing too hard for God!

LIVING IT

Devon's life isn't easy. His dad left when he was just a little boy and his mom has to work hard just to have enough money for food and to pay for a little apartment for them to live in. Devon sees how hard she works and he doesn't think things are ever going to get better for them.

But then he reads that nothing is impossible for God – nothing on earth and nothing in heaven. So, he trusts God to take care of them and to invite them into His heaven someday.

> "If that is how God clothes the grass of the field, which is here today, and tomorrow is thrown into the fire, how much more will He clothe you, O you of little faith!"
> Luke 12:28

Terrible things happen around the world every day – earthquakes, hurricanes, tsunamis, floods and wars. You may be facing some tough things yourself.

Do you ever wonder whether God cares? He does care but He doesn't always show that care by taking away the problems. He doesn't make us go through them alone though. God cares a lot more for His children than He does about the grass and we see that He makes the grass beautifully green.

Trust Him to be with you regardless of how tough life is. He will. He loves you.

LIVING IT

Alan isn't so sure about this. It doesn't really feel like God is taking care of things sometimes. He gets pretty discouraged and even scared sometimes.

When Alan talked to his dad about his feelings, his dad helped him talk through all the ways God takes care of them every day. It really helped Alan to make a list of the ways God cares for him. It helped him learn to trust God more with the things that scare him.

YOUR ASSIGNMENT IS ...

> "Go into all the world and preach the good news to all creation."
>
> Mark 16:15

God's greatest desire is that everyone in the whole world would come to know Him. He wants everyone to be saved. That's a big desire and can only happen with a lot of teamwork.

You are a part of that team who must tell others about His love. Jesus said to go and tell everyone the good news of His love and His plan for salvation.

All of us who know Him have been given that command.

LIVING IT

So, how does someone your age preach the good news? Do you get nervous when you try to talk about something so important? Maybe you don't feel qualified to preach like your pastor. That's OK – not everyone can do that.

However, there is one thing you are really good at – being you. So, you can obey Jesus' command by just being yourself and being a good friend who lets God's love flow through you. You can be an example of God's kindness, love and concern to all your friends!

> "This is My command: Love each other."
> John 15:17

OK – you're a guy. You don't like to talk about love. But, Jesus isn't just talking about love between a guy and a girl. Love is Jesus' basic message. He tells us many times to love one another. He even tells us to love our enemies.

Jesus wanted people to get along. Wow, if everyone obeyed Him, imagine what a nicer world we would live in. There would be no hate, no murders, no crime at all. People would help each other and listen to each other – even when they disagreed.

How wonderful would that be? Love. Just do it.

LIVING IT

Ryan is a great athlete, a star pitcher on his baseball team and popular in his class. There is a guy in his class who has lots of issues. He is in a wheelchair, doesn't learn very quickly and can't talk very well.

Most kids ignore him. But Ryan doesn't. In fact, he goes out of his way to hang out with Michael on the playground and to sit by him at lunch. Ryan goes out of his way to love Michael even though others do not. Ryan is an example of Jesus' love to Michael.

FORGIVING OVER AND OVER

"If your brother sins, rebuke him, and if he repents, forgive him. If he sins against you seven times in a day, and seven times comes back to you and says, 'I repent,' forgive him."

Luke 17:3-4

One time Jesus was asked how many times you have to forgive someone who hurts you. His answer was, "Over and over and over." In other words – don't keep count.

God forgives our sins day after day and we should be willing to do the same for others. When a friend apologizes for something he did we shouldn't even have to think twice about forgiving.

Forgive and forgive and forgive. That's what love does.

LIVING IT

Kevin is not so good at forgiving. He's good at keeping score. He keeps score of how his friends treat him and then he is super good at getting even with them if they treat him badly. He likes to win. Kevin doesn't give anyone a second chance. Once you hurt Kevin you are pushed to the outside of his circle of friends. Kevin needs to learn how to forgive in the same way God forgives him ... over and over. God never pushes Kevin out just because he hurts or disobeys Him. Come on, Kevin, be more like God – forgive and forgive!

January 24

BE A PEACEMAKER

"Blessed are the peace-makers, for they will be called sons of God."
Matthew 5:9

Some guys think they are always right so they argue about everything. These guys always have to win and even on the smallest point they will argue till the other guys give in. Guys like this don't have a lot of true friends.

On the flip side is the guy who tries to keep peace between others. He doesn't argue about everything and he tries to find bridges between other people's differences so he can help settle their fights.

This kind of guy is a peacemaker. That is what God wants all His children to be.

LIVING IT

No one would accuse Todd of being a peacemaker. Hah! Most guys are even careful about what they say to him because they know whatever it is, he will have a different opinion and he will be right! At least he will only argue until they give in just to get away from him! Yeah, Todd has a lot to learn about being a peacemaker.

Stop arguing. You don't always have to be right. Be a bridge between others. Think about others before yourself.

THE PROUD GO DOWN

> "Whoever exalts himself will be humbled, and whoever humbles himself will be exalted."
>
> Matthew 23:12

Jesus doesn't think much of people who are full of pride and brag about themselves all the time.

Well, the truth is that no one believes what the bragger says except the one doing the bragging anyway. The guy who is full of pride needs to realize that none of us could do anything if God hadn't given us our abilities.

God is the only one who has any right to brag! Jesus encourages us to be humble and to help others to shine.

The humble person will be respected by others and have God's approval. Be humble – it's the God way!

LIVING IT

Jack is the life of the party! Everyone loves hanging out with him because he is fun, full of jokes, really smart and a great athlete. Well, to be truthful there isn't much that Jack isn't good at.

But, you would never know that by talking with him. He never brags about anything and often finds encouraging things to say to others. He celebrates every one of their successes. That's probably why everyone likes Jack.

January 26

IMPORTANT CONVERSATIONS

> "Your Father knows what you need before you ask Him."
> Matthew 6:8

What would you say if you could talk to a world leader or a star athlete or the leader of a big company? Would you be able to say anything at all? Well, think about this – you can actually talk to the Creator of the universe!

Prayer is a privilege you have to talk with God. You can tell Him what you're scared about; what you need and what you hope for.

God promises to hear your prayers and to answer them with what He knows is best for you. He can see the whole picture of your life and He knows exactly what you need, even before you know that you need it!

God loves you very much so you can trust Him to take care of you!

LIVING IT

Lawrence is a big baseball fan and has one favorite player. He sometimes daydreams about meeting this famous athlete and what he might say to him. He knows, though, that if he did meet the guy he would probably get so nervous he wouldn't be able to talk at all.

Funny that Lawrence never thinks about being nervous when he talks to God ... and he shouldn't be nervous! God wants to hear from him and cares about everything Lawrence says to Him. God loves him and wants to answer his prayers!

January 27

LIGHT THAT SHOWS EVERYTHING!

> "Everyone who does evil hates the light, and will not come into the light for fear that his deeds will be exposed."
>
> John 3:20

The bad things some people do cannot be hidden forever! Jesus is the Light of the world. When He gets close to you His light shows the sin in your life.

When you know that you have sinned then you can confess it, ask forgiveness for it and change how you are living.

But, a person who doesn't want to stop doing sinful things will not want to be "in the light" or close to Jesus. He won't want the sinful things he does to show – even to himself.

LIVING IT

Corey seems to think that the things he does that no one else knows about are not really sin. Boy is he in for a surprise! God knows everything Corey does so there really are no secret sins!

Once Corey realizes that the light of Jesus shows everything, even the things hidden away in the dark, he will be more honest about his "secret sins" and face the truth.

LIFE-GIVING WATER!

"Everyone who drinks this water will be thirsty again, but whoever drinks the water I give him will never thirst. Indeed, the water I give him will become in him a spring of water welling up to eternal life."

John 4:13-14

People are born with a thirst to be loved and to know that their lives matter. People try to quench this thirst in many ways.

Some try money. Some try a powerful career or even fame. As they get older, some try alcohol or drugs. Those things don't work. You might feel better for a half a second, but then the loneliness and lack of purpose comes back.

The only thing that will quench that thirst forever is Jesus. He lasts for eternity.

LIVING IT

Have you named that thirst in your heart ... the desire to be loved and to know that your life matters? Maybe money, career or fame doesn't mean much at your age. Hopefully the alcohol and drugs route just seems dumb.

So, what will quench the thirst? Even if you achieve your dreams, the feeling of fulfillment will be temporary. That's obvious from the celebrities who have everything they could want, but say they really aren't happy. The only thing that will give purpose to your life is Jesus.

CELEBRATE THE CHILDREN!

> "Let the little children come to Me, and do not hinder them, for the kingdom of God belongs to such as these."
>
> Mark 10:14

Some of Jesus' followers didn't think He should make time for children. They tried to get kids to leave Him alone, but He said, "Let them come!"

Why did He say that God's kingdom belongs to people who are like children? Because children trust and don't argue about every point or need to have things proven to them.

As people grow up they sometimes lose that childlike trust. Childlike faith is much more pleasing to God because it is a faith that just trusts Him.

LIVING IT

It's nice to hear something good about being a kid. Since you are young, you hopefully still have the kind of faith that just trusts God. But as life gets more complicated, that childlike faith gets harder to hold on to and you start asking lots of questions.

When that happens your trust in God slips once in a while. Try not to let that happen. Start today on making your faith as strong as possible so that your trust will remain childlike as you grow up.

January 30

> "Love your enemies, do good to those who hate you, bless those who curse you, pray for those who mistreat you."
>
> Luke 6:27-28

You love your friends. Big deal. It's easy to love people who love you back. The real test of loving like Jesus is whether you can love people who bully you, say mean things or just generally treat you badly.

Can you love them? Can you pray for them even if they don't want your prayers and kindness?

That's the kind of love Jesus is talking about here.

LIVING IT

OK, Will wouldn't really say that he "loves" his friends. He does, but he probably wouldn't say that. Love isn't the word he would use, but he enjoys his friends and likes hanging out with them. He would defend, support and stand up for his friends, no matter what.

He also knows guys that are mean and he wouldn't support or defend them at all! But, according to Jesus he should. The guys he doesn't like so much are the very ones he should defend and support. Gulp. Not easy, but Jesus will help him.

January 31

WORTH MORE THAN A BIRD

> "Are not two sparrows sold for a penny? Yet not one of them will fall to the ground apart from the will of your Father."
>
> Matthew 10:29

Most people don't think about everyday birds, after all you see dozens of them every day. Sparrows are common, ordinary birds. They are really nothing special in the bird world; except to God. He made them.

God knows what is happening with every bit of His creation so even plain old sparrows matter to Him.

Nothing happens to God's stuff without God having a hand in it. So a simple bird can't fall from the sky without God deciding on that action.

Yep, He is in control of everything in your life! Cool, eh?

LIVING IT

Mark has had a tough time lately. His mom and dad split up and his dad moved away. Mark misses his dad a lot. His mom is sad and doesn't pay as much attention to him as she used to. Mark feels invisible. He wonders if anyone really cares what happens to him.

At least, he used to feel that way, until he read these verses in Matthew. When Mark thinks about God paying that much attention to little birds, it's easier to believe that He really cares about him and knows what's going on in his life.

BROWN SUGAR

How good are chocolate chip cookies right out of the oven? Yum. Have you ever made chocolate chip cookies?

Brown sugar is one ingredient of that recipe. You put brown sugar in the measuring cup, press it down and add more, press it down again and add more. It's amazing how much sugar you can get in a measuring cup.

Guess what? That's how God's blessings are to people who are generous. When you give, God gives, too. He just gives and gives and gives. You cannot out-give God!

LIVING IT

Chocolate chip cookies are Mason's favorite. Sometimes he helps his mom make them and she lets him press brown sugar into the measuring cup. Mason has also seen this verse in action in his grandpa's life. Gramps helps anyone who needs help. He fixes things for the neighbors. He mows grass for a friend who hurt his back. He volunteers at a hospital. Gramps is awesome! It seems like the more Gramps gives, the more he gets back in the form of friendships, help from people and just pure joy. It's proof for Mason that you can never out-give God!

February 2

LET YOUR LIGHT SHINE!

"Let your light shine before men, that they may see your good deeds and praise your Father in heaven."

Matthew 5:16

What light is Jesus talking about in this verse? Earlier in Matthew Jesus called Himself the Light of the world. So, it makes sense that when you accept Jesus into your heart, His light shines inside you.

Jesus completed the light instruction with – **let it shine**! When people know that you are a Christian and they see the light of Jesus in your actions they give credit to God.

Your light is a witness to God's love and power!

LIVING IT

James knows that his actions might make his buddies think about God. He is serious about living for God so he keeps in mind that his words, the jokes he makes, the things he does, the ways he treats people – all those things will either draw his buddies to God or push them away.

February 3

HEARING ISN'T GOOD ENOUGH

If you hear a lesson taught but don't believe what you hear then it doesn't sink into your heart and become a part of your values.

Just hearing God's Word is not enough. Sometimes people hear the message of God's love, but they don't let it sink into their hearts so they don't give themselves a chance to really believe it.

That gives Satan a chance to sneak in and steal that word away. Then their faith in God never takes root and grows.

"Some people are like seed along the path, where the word is sown. As soon as they hear it, Satan comes and takes away the word that was sown in them."

Mark 4:15

LIVING IT

Jackson is a really fun guy. His friends love being around him because they know something crazy will surely happen. Jackson's parents have taken him to church since he was a little boy. So, he has heard the message of God's love and how Jesus died for his sins. He has heard it, but he hasn't believed it.

Hearing it isn't enough. Jackson is not a member of God's family yet. He must believe and then act on what he believes by inviting Jesus into his heart!

February 4

HARVEST WORKERS

> "The harvest is plentiful, but the workers are few. Ask the Lord of the harvest, therefore, to send out workers into His harvest field."
>
> Luke 10:2

The world is full of people who don't know about Jesus' love. There are many people who would accept Jesus if someone would just tell them about Him. They can't respond to something they haven't heard!

Jesus challenges His followers to do their part in telling others in the world about His love. Missionaries leave home and go to other parts of the world to tell of God's love.

Some people give money to help those who go. Some people pray for the missionaries.

Each one has a part in the harvest of those who come to Jesus.

LIVING IT

Michael thinks it's great that missionaries travel around the world to tell others of God's love. But it's not something he feels called to do, at least at this point in his life. Michael has friends and classmates who do not know Jesus. He can be a missionary to them.

Michael isn't really comfortable talking about Jesus yet, but he can live his life with kindness and love and respect for others and give the credit to Jesus. His kindness will be a testimony of Jesus' work in his life and his friends may come to Jesus just because of that!

February 5

THE LOVE OF GOD'S FAMILY

"By this all men will know that you are My disciples, if you love one another."

John 13:35

Why do some people try to solve problems by fighting? It doesn't ever really work.

There's no room in Jesus' family for arguing or fighting. When you think about it, if the members of Jesus' family can't get along with each other, why would others want to be a part of it?

Jesus' followers should be united by their love for Him and their love for one another. So, don't let little things come between you and other Christians. Solve your differences quickly and let love be your guide.

LIVING IT

Jude and Brody are brothers who are only about a year apart in age. Sometimes they play together and have fun. But more often they are wrestling or tackling each other and often end up fighting. But, if someone else picks on one of them the other one steps up and defends his brother because they really do love each other. Just like a human family, members of God's family may tussle some, but the bottom line is that they love one another and will take care of one another in any way they can. That shows God's love to everyone else!

February 6

> "Away from Me, Satan! For it is written: 'Worship the Lord your God, and serve Him only!'"
> Matthew 4:10

Satan thought he could get Jesus to worship him instead of God. After being tempted, Jesus told Satan to go away. He said the Scriptures say to worship God and serve only Him.

There are a couple of things to notice here. One is that Jesus knew what was written in Scripture. If it's important enough for Jesus to know then you should know what is in Scripture, too, right?

The second thing is that Jesus declared that God should be more important than anything else. Worship only God!

LIVING IT

Calvin is crazy about music. He plays drums and guitar and just about any other instrument he picks up. Pretty much all his time is spent practicing, listening to music or talking about music. Calvin lets music rule his life. It's more important to him than God. He spends way more time on music than he does reading the Bible or praying or even thinking about God.

So, what's the most important thing to Calvin? God or music? OK, so what does Calvin worship? Yeah, that's an eye-opener! Time to make some adjustments in his life, right?

SHARING THE WEALTH

"It is easier for a camel to go through the eye of a needle than for a rich man to enter the kingdom of God."

Mark 10:25

Jesus was speaking to a rich young man who wanted to know what he had to do to be saved. Jesus told him to give away all his money. Whoa! The rich man just couldn't do that.

Now, there's nothing wrong with being rich. But sometimes money becomes more important to people than God. Sometimes wealthy people don't think they need anyone's help, even God's. They think money can solve all their problems.

A person who trusts God and depends on Him will find it easy to enter the kingdom of God.

LIVING IT

Sam doesn't think he needs anyone's help. He's a tough guy and his parents have enough money to get him whatever he wants. They have a nice home, lots of expensive stuff, take exciting vacations and Sam has everything he could want. Sam thinks that he doesn't need God. What Sam hasn't realized yet is that God loves him and what He can give Sam is something money can't buy – purpose in his life and a future in heaven. But, Sam has to trust God and depend on Him as he admits that yes, he needs God!

February 8

A DIFFERENT KIND OF FISHING

> "Don't be afraid; from now on you will catch men."
> Luke 5:10

Several of Jesus' first disciples were fishermen before they started following Him. That's how they earned their livings.

When Jesus called them to follow Him, He explained what their future held in ways they would understand.

When Jesus said they would be catching men, He was saying they would now be winning people to faith in Him. That would be their new career – fishing for souls!

LIVING IT

Ryan is a fisherman. He easily puts bait on a hook and then puts it in the water to attract fish. So, he understands that by sharing God's love with people, he is catching men for God because they have the chance to accept Jesus.

Ryan understands that the mission of God's people is to share the story of His love with others. When others hear how much He loves them, they have the chance to accept Him as Savior. So, Ryan understands that by sharing God's love he is "catching men" for Him! Ryan is happy to be that kind of fisherman!

February 9

LOUDER THAN WORDS

"If you love Me, you will obey what I command."
John 14:15

You can say that you love God. You can even think that you mean it. You certainly want to love Him. But, while saying you love Him and wanting to love Him is the first step, the real proof that you do love Him is shown when you obey Jesus' teachings.

They are all written down for you in the Bible so you can't say, "I would obey them but I don't know them."

If you say you love God, show it by reading His Word, learning His commands and obeying them.

LIVING IT

Matthew says he loves Jesus. He reads his Bible and prays every day. He is kind to others. When he hurts someone, he is quick to apologize. He is honest. He sacrifices for others by helping them when he would rather play and by cheering for a friend who gets an honor that Matthew wanted.

Aaron says he loves Jesus. He doesn't read his Bible, pray, help others, or cheer for anyone. Aaron thinks only about Aaron and feels he deserves the best of everything. Which one obeys Jesus' commands?

> "When you give to the needy, do not announce it with trumpets, as the hypocrites do in the synagogues and on the streets, to be honored by men. I tell you the truth, they have received their reward in full."
>
> Matthew 6:2

Giving to the poor is a good thing to do. In fact, it's what Jesus said to do.

However, bragging about your generosity so that others pat you on the back and compliment you does not please God.

A guy who gives to the needy just so others will notice and think, "Wow, he is generous!" will not be rewarded by God. The pats on the back he receives are all the reward he gets!

LIVING IT

Robbie wants to play baseball this summer but since his dad lost his job there isn't any extra money in their family and the registration fee is kind of high. Robbie has pretty much given up on the possibility of playing.

Then one day an envelope appeared in their mailbox addressed to Robbie. It had just enough money in it to pay for team registration! There was no note, no return address, just money. So Robbie doesn't even know who shared this generous gift, but God knows!

February 11

ONE SPECIAL SHEEP

"What do you think? If a man owns a hundred sheep, and one of them wanders away, will he not leave the ninety-nine on the hills and go to look for the one that wandered off?"

Matthew 18:12

Would you think that a man who had 100 sheep wouldn't even notice if one of them got lost? And, if he did, wouldn't it be more important to stay with the 99 sheep and keep them safe than to go look for the lost one?

Well, this is an illustration of how much God loves **you**! He would do anything to find you and bring you into His family.

God's love is greater than anything!

LIVING IT

Sam's dad left the family when he was only 6 years old. Since then Sam has never felt special. He misses his dad and he often wonders why his dad didn't love him enough to stick around.

Sam often feels kind of lost. When he heard this story about the shepherd searching for one lost sheep he wondered if he was like that sheep, and if God would search for him.

As he thought about it he realized that Jesus loves **him** very much. Sam feels pretty special now.

February 12

"What is the kingdom of God like? What shall I compare it to? It is like a mustard seed, which a man took and planted in his garden. It grew and became a tree, and the birds of the air perched in its branches."

Luke 13:18-19

Jesus often compared God's kingdom to things that people knew about. He did that so they would understand how wonderful heaven is.

The people He was speaking with here knew what a mustard seed was. They knew that it is a tiny seed.

God's kingdom starts small, too – in a single heart. But it grows and grows into many hearts.

By the time Jesus returns to take His children to heaven the kingdom will be bigger and more wonderful than you can imagine. It will be everything you can dream of.

LIVING IT

Jon asked Jesus to be his Savior and he is very serious about telling everyone he knows that God loves them and that Jesus died for them.

Jon does everything he can to grow God's kingdom. The message of God's love started as a small seed in his heart, but it grows and grows every day as he shares it with others.

February 13

JUST DO IT!

"If anyone causes one of these little ones who believe in Me to sin, it would be better for him to be thrown into the sea with a large millstone tied around his neck."

Mark 9:42

Sin is serious business. Jesus makes that clear. If a guy leads another Christian into sin on purpose, he's in big trouble.

Jesus says that the one who caused the sin is responsible for his own sin **and** the sin of the other person, too!

Take seriously the command not to sin and to take care of one another so that you don't lead others into sin.

Pay attention!

LIVING IT

"Dude, it's fun. Come on, just do it," Rob urged. But, Eric wasn't so sure. "Just throw the rock. If you hit a window it's a point for you. Come on, no one lives there. It's no big deal!"

Eric knew what Rob was doing was wrong, but he didn't want Rob to think he was chicken. Rob was doing exactly what Jesus said NOT to do – leading someone else to sin. There's no doubt he will answer to God for this.

February 14

> "Whoever believes in Him is not condemned, but whoever does not believe stands condemned already because He has not believed in the name of God's one and only Son."
>
> John 3:18

Jesus made it clear that there is one way to heaven and one way only.

To be saved you must believe that Jesus is God's only Son, and that Jesus did not sin at all, but came to earth and died for your sins so that your heart could be cleansed of its sins.

God brought Jesus back to life and now He is alive waiting to spend forever with you in heaven. If you don't believe this, you are condemned – you will not be allowed into heaven – you will be separated from God forever. Plain and simple.

LIVING IT

Mark plans to accept Jesus someday, probably when he is older. He knows that Jesus is God's Son, but he figures he will have plenty of time to think about serious stuff like that when he is older.

It's not a good idea to put off something when you know it is the right thing to do. Being separated from God is no fun. Mark should act right now on what he knows is right.

THE PAIN OF MOURNING

> "Blessed are those who mourn, for they will be comforted."
> Matthew 5:4

Being sad is ... sad. But mourning is more than being sad. Mourning is when your heart aches because you are so sad.

Jesus promises comfort for you when you are mourning. The comfort comes from God's love for you, His care for you and because He brings other loved ones into your life to help you.

He does that because He loves you.

LIVING IT

Phil is sad and a little bit scared, too. Everything in his world has changed. His dad is a soldier and ... well, he won't be coming home from the war. What's going to happen to Phil and his mother? Who will take care of them? And, besides that, Phil misses his dad very much.

Phil is way beyond sad – he is mourning. His comfort will come only from knowing how much God loves him and that God will take care of him and his mom.

"When you pray, do not be like the hypocrites, for they love to pray standing in the synagogues and on the street corners to be seen by men. I tell you the truth, they have received their reward in full."

Matthew 6:5

Jesus often instructed people to do things in private. Praying is an important part of our relationship with Jesus, but is not meant to be a show for others.

Jesus said that to put on a big show of praying just so other people will think you are super spiritual actually makes you look like someone who is only pretending to know Jesus.

Prayer is private – between you and Him – even when you're praying in a group. Don't try to impress others with your prayers, just talk to Jesus.

LIVING IT

Andrew thinks that he might want to be a pastor someday. He feels that God has placed that desire on his heart. Once in a while he gets caught up with what his future might hold and he wants his friends to know that he loves Jesus and feels God's call on his life. He is tempted to stand up in Sunday school and pray out loud – long, fancy prayers. But, doing that just so others think he is somehow more spiritual than they are would be wrong – as this verse says. Praying for show doesn't win you any super spiritual awards! Just pray from your heart.

BEWARE!

> "I tell you that to everyone who has, more will be given, but as for the one who has nothing, even what he has will be taken away."
>
> Luke 19:26

What kind of worker are you? When you are given a job do you take it seriously and give it your best?

Did you know that everyone in God's family has a job? The cool thing is that God gives you exactly what you need to do that job. Each talent, skill or ability you have is a gift from Him. He wants you to use it to honor Him and share His love with others.

However, if a guy chooses not to use what God has given him or to use it for some purpose other than honoring Him ... **beware** ... that talent and ability may be taken away!

LIVING IT

Tyler is an awesome guitar player. He is often asked to help lead worship at church and youth group. He is also asked to go places with different ministries of the church – refugee ministry, nursing home ministry, outreach and play the guitar.

Tyler knows that his ability is a gift from God and he gives the glory for it back to God. So, he is happy to play guitar for pretty much anyone who asks. He is giving his gift back to God!

> "Do not work for food that spoils, but for food that endures to eternal life, which the Son of Man will give you. On Him God the Father has placed His seal of approval."
>
> John 6:27

Food is pretty important, right? Yeah, you need it to live. People work to earn money for food. A lot of time, energy and money are spent on food. But there is something even more important than cheeseburgers and fries and that is knowing and serving God.

Jesus encouraged people to put their energy and focus on that kind of food – spiritual food.

Learn to know God by reading His Word and by serving and obeying Him. That will give you "food" that lasts forever.

LIVING IT

Rick sees two types of people in his family. Both types provide food for their families, so that isn't an issue. But Uncle Rob puts all his energy into earning more and more money. He buys bigger cars, and fancier houses. He just wants more and more stuff. God isn't important to him at all.

But, Uncle Tim is serious about God. He gives lots of time and money to people who need help. He reads his Bible, prays and serves God. Uncle Tim provides food for his earthly family now and he is laying up food in heaven, too.

A HUMBLE EXAMPLE

> "I have set you an example that you should do as I have done for you."
>
> John 13:15

Sometimes it's easier to learn to do things if you have an example to follow.

Jesus doesn't ask His followers to live in a way that is impossible. We know that because His life is a model for how to live. All we have to do is follow His example of humble service.

Do you need proof? Jesus said this right after He washed His disciples' feet. That was a humble job to do – a job usually done by a servant. By washing their feet, Jesus showed His followers how to serve others humbly and quietly.

LIVING IT

Michael doesn't even have to think about what to do. When someone needs help and he can help, Michael just gets busy and does whatever he can.

He is happy to help others by mowing lawns, pulling weeds, running errands, playing with young kids so their moms can get work done. Michael will do anything and do it without bragging. He likes to serve others just as Jesus did.

THE HOLY SPIRIT

"I will ask the Father, and He will give you another Counselor to be with you forever – the Spirit of truth."
John 14:16-17

This is such an awesome promise from Jesus because the Counselor, the Spirit of truth is the Holy Spirit.

Jesus promised the Holy Spirit to His followers. God sent Him to live in our hearts. Since He is in our hearts all the time, He helps us know right from wrong. He guides us to know what is true and right.

If you ever wonder if something is right or wrong just ask God to show you and the Spirit will help you know!

LIVING IT

Craig lives a couple of houses down from Jay. They have a good time together and like to do a lot of the same things. But one afternoon when Jay went over to shoot baskets with Craig they ended up hanging out in Craig's room. He dove under his bed and pulled out a magazine, and shoved it at Jay. "Look at this, Dude. It's hot!" he said. Jay got a glimpse of the woman on the cover and knew it wasn't something he should look at. He shot off a quick prayer for guidance of what to say. The Holy Spirit gave him the answer: "Nah, it's gonna be dark soon. Let's go shoot hoops while we can!" he said.

February 21

GIVE YOUR ALL

> "They all gave out of their wealth; but she, out of her poverty, put in everything – all she had to live on."
>
> Mark 12:44

Jesus compared a rich man who gave lots of money to God's work to a widow who gave a couple of pennies.

He said that even though she didn't give much, she did give all she had. Jesus admired the woman because she held nothing back from God.

The rich man actually gave more money, but it was his extra money not money he needed to live. The widow gave everything.

Jesus looks at the heart of the giver and notices how much he holds back for himself compared with how much he is willing to give to others.

LIVING IT

Tim is saving money to buy a new pair of ice skates. He is a great hockey player, but knows he would be even more awesome if he got better skates. He thinks he could be the team star! He was really close to having enough money when he heard about children on an Indian reservation in North Dakota who didn't have clean water to drink. Tim couldn't get the thought of them out of his mind. *Everyone should have clean water to drink*, he thought. Do you know what Tim did? He gave all of his money to a ministry working to send water to the children!

> "I tell you that unless your righteousness surpasses that of the Pharisees and the teachers of the law, you will certainly not enter the kingdom of heaven."
>
> Matthew 5:20

The Pharisees and teachers of the law were the religious leaders of Jesus' day. They should have been the most righteous and the best ones at knowing and obeying Jesus' teachings. But they weren't.

Instead they decided for themselves what was important and they obeyed those laws. They even made up their own rules and insisted that other people obey them. But, they didn't obey some of the most important laws of God – for example loving others!

LIVING IT

"I don't like rules!" Patrick moaned, "and Christianity is just a bunch of rules. I don't need that! I can make my own decisions!"

The problem is that Patrick has been criticized by some Christians who think that everyone has to live by a bunch of rules that don't make any sense. There isn't much room for love in their lives.

Patrick needs to meet Christians who know how to love the way God teaches.

THE BEST WAY

"Enter through the narrow gate. For wide is the gate and broad is the road that leads to destruction, and many enter through it."

Matthew 7:13

Some people would say that the easy way is the best way.

Jesus noticed that many people choose the easy way through life – at least it appears to be the easy way.

It may seem that the wide road is the best way because it seems to have less rules and gives you more control over your own life. However, the narrow way is the one that leads to God.

That road takes you to love, care and protection. The door to the narrow way is opened by Jesus.

LIVING IT

Jackson does not take the easy way in anything he does. He works hard at school. He practices hard at music and sports. He takes on challenges with courage. Even when Jackson is a little scared about the challenges he faces, he knows he can be brave because Jesus is with him. When someone says that his choice to obey Jesus looks hard, Jackson says, "No way!" He knows that the description of the narrow way doesn't mean harder it means better because it leads to Jesus and the joy of knowing Him.

February 24

> "Ask and it will be given to you; seek and you will find; knock and the door will be opened to you."
> Matthew 7:7

Do you have a buddy that you really like to talk with? Maybe you have the same hobby and you can spend hours talking about things that interest you.

Talking with someone is the way you get to know him better and you get to be closer friends.

Well, guess what? Jesus wants you to talk to Him. He wants to hear what you need and how you feel.

You have the privilege of talking to Him in prayer. Tell Him what you need. Tell Him how you feel. Just talk with Jesus.

LIVING IT

Rob and Ryan can spend hours talking about cars; especially race cars. They both love Nascar and are fascinated by the talents of the race car drivers. Their friendship has gotten stronger because of those conversations. They've gotten to know each other better. Both know what the other likes and even how the other thinks.

These conversations have helped Rob and Ryan understand how important conversation is and that their conversations with Jesus help them get to know Him better and help Him to know them. Prayer is important.

February 25

SOURCE OF LIFE

"I am the true vine, and My Father is the gardener."
John 15:1

Jesus is the source of all life. If you know anything about plants you know that a vine brings food to its leaves and flowers through its roots.

In much the same way Jesus brings nutrition to His children. He gives them the power and strength to grow and be healthy and strong. He is the connection to God, the Father of all things.

Jesus made this statement to encourage His followers to stay close to Him so they could get the nutrition they need to grow.

LIVING IT

Kent loves junk food. He could live on French fries and cookies if his mom would let him. But, his mom helps him understand that junk food does not make his body grow strong. It makes his body fat and gives him no energy or strength. Good nutrition makes a strong body and a strong brain. Kent has learned that Jesus does the same thing for his heart so he stays close to Him by reading his Bible and talking to Him in prayer. If he puts junk in his heart, then his heart is kind of dirty. The closer Kent stays to Jesus, the healthier his heart is!

"In the same way, I tell you, there is rejoicing in the presence of the angels of God over one sinner who repents."
Luke 15:10

Just in case you ever begin to feel that you do not matter to God, go back and read this verse. Read it again and again.

Jesus said this after talking about how a woman looked everywhere to find one little lost coin.

When she found it all her friends came and celebrated with her!

Jesus loves YOU so much that when you repented of your sins and accepted Him as Savior, there was a paaarrrtttyyyy in heaven!

LIVING IT

It would feel awesome to be special to someone, Bradley thought. He didn't feel special though; not to anyone for any reason. His family was kind of messed up. He thought his mom probably loved him, but she didn't say so very often. He wasn't extra good at anything. He was just average.

But, when Bradley thinks about the residents of heaven throwing a party in his honor, well, then he KNOWS that he is special to God!

BIG TALKER

> "These people honor Me with their lips, but their hearts are far from Me."
>
> Mark 7:6

These words are from the book of Isaiah in the Old Testament. Jesus is quoting from it. Why is that important? Because it shows that Jesus knew the Scriptures. If that was important for Jesus, it no doubt is important for you, too.

The message is that worshiping and honoring Jesus comes from your heart that wants to do those things.

You can say all the right words but if your heart honors something or someone else, Jesus will know it. He sees your heart.

LIVING IT

Noah has all the answers about pretty much everything. He's loud and pushy about spouting his opinions. He almost brags about how much he knows about the Bible. He can list the Ten Commandments and a whole bunch of other "rules" from the Bible.

It sounds like Noah is a serious Christ-follower, but Jesus sees his heart. Noah has not even asked Jesus to be his Savior. His heart belongs to a lot of other things – not God. People may be fooled by Noah's talk, but Jesus is not.

> "My Father is always at his work to this very day, and I, too, am working."
>
> John 5:17

God never goes on vacation. He never takes a day off. God and Jesus are always paying attention to what is going on in the world and to you!

This verse shows that God and Jesus are one. They both have the goal of bringing people into God's family and teaching, guiding and loving them.

You never have to worry about whether God knows what you're dealing with. He does. Nothing surprises Him!

LIVING IT

Brad's dad lost his job. He now has a few possibilities for a new job, but the scary thing is that it might mean that the family has to move. Brad is scared about that because it would mean leaving his friends and his school.

But, this verse promises him that God is always working. So he can trust Him to take care of things. Brad has to remember that God does things in His own time and He will take care of Brad and any situations that develop. Whatever happens.

MARCH

LOVE YOUR ENEMIES

"If you love those who love you, what credit is that to you? Even 'sinners' love those who love them."

Luke 6:32

Do you love your friends and family? Of course, you do! But, Jesus said that isn't enough.

He wants you to love people you don't know and even love people who are mean to you. Being able to do that is what sets you apart from people who don't know God.

It's not easy though. So how do you do it?

There is only one way – let God love through you. He'll do the hard work, just let Him.

LIVING IT

Michael gets along well with most people. But he has very little patience for one guy he knows. Todd is pushy and opinionated and treats other kids very badly. He just isn't very nice. Michael knows what Jesus says about loving people who aren't nice to you. So, yeah, he should love Todd ... but it isn't easy.

The only way is for Michael to ask God to love Todd through him. Then when Michael has mean thoughts about Todd he can ask God to take them away and help him love Todd. Guess what? It works!

March 1

BETTER FRUIT

"By their fruit you will recognize them. Do people pick grapes from thornbushes, or figs from thistles?"
Matthew 7:16

When you go to an apple orchard, what kind of fruit do you plan to pick? Apples, right? Apple trees don't grow oranges or bananas. That's just silly.

In this verse Jesus is explaining that just like trees are known by what fruit they grow, people are known by how they live their lives.

So, a person who claims to know Jesus will live a life that honors Him. The "fruit" of a Jesus-follower's life will be love for Him and others and service to Him.

LIVING IT

"CHEATER! You are nothing but a cheat!" David hears those words a lot from friends because they are true. He cheats in sports. He cheats in board games. He cheats all the time. It's like he can't help himself. David says that he loves Jesus. But, the "fruit" of his life doesn't match what should grow in the life of a Jesus-follower.

David needs to confess his sin, ask forgiveness and then get serious about his life showing that he does love Jesus! He needs better fruit!

March 2

> "What comes out of a man is what makes him 'unclean.'"
>
> Mark 7:20

Nothing goes better with fresh-from-the-oven chocolate chip cookies than a glass of cold milk.

But what if you open a fresh carton of milk, take a bite from a cookie and a gulp of milk and ... **yuck!** It's sour and tastes awful!

You see, the package looked really cool, but what came out of the package showed that the product was no good.

Jesus said that a person can look really cool from the outside, but what comes out of him – his behavior, the way he treats others, his words – those things show that his heart is unclean if they do not honor God.

LIVING IT

Bill is trouble waiting to happen. He picks fights with other kids. He is disrespectful to his mom and dad. He bullies his little brother. He is just not a nice guy.

The problem is that Bill has not asked Jesus into his heart so Jesus hasn't cleaned the wickedness out of it. What comes out of Bill – his words and his behavior – shows just how unclean he is on the inside. Yeah, Bill needs Jesus!

AN IMPORTANT COMMAND

> "A new command I give you: Love one another. As I have loved you, so you must love one another."
>
> John 13:34

Jesus wants all of His followers to love one another.

If we can't get along with each other what makes us any different from those who do not know Jesus?

He said to love one another as He loved us. What does that mean? He loved us so much that He died for us. That means we should love one another and show our love by giving of our time, energy, priorities – whatever others need.

LIVING IT

Love one another. That doesn't sound like such a tough thing to do ... except it is sometimes. When friends make you mad, tell lies about you or don't support you, then it's kind of hard to love. Sometimes there is a big competition between friends and then it's hard to love, too.

Jesus said to work those things out and find a way to love one another. It matters because others are watching how you, as God's people, love one another.

March 4

> "Don't be afraid; just believe."
> Mark 5:36

What makes you afraid? What do you do when you are scared? Did you know that you can trust Jesus to take care of you?

No matter what problems life brings, you can trust in His power and strength.

Jesus spoke these words to a father who had just been told that his daughter was dead.

Imagine hearing Jesus say not to be afraid but trust Him when someone you love very much has just died. But, the father did trust Jesus and his trust paid off.

There is nothing Jesus can't handle. Nothing.

LIVING IT

Sammy tries very hard to draw no attention to himself when he is at home. His dad is mean and thinks nothing of slapping Sammy against a wall or even beating him until he bleeds. Sammy doesn't know what might set his dad off on any night. Usually there isn't much reason for the beatings. Sammy is scared of his dad.

He wants to believe that Jesus will take care of him and protect him from his dad. Believing is hard, but he is learning more each day how to do it.

JESUS MEETS YOUR NEEDS

> "I tell you the truth, you are looking for Me, not because you saw miraculous signs but because you ate the loaves and had your fill."
>
> John 6:26

Jesus knew that some people hung out with Him just for the miracles they thought He could do for them.

Today some people still view Jesus as a giant Santa Claus in the sky. Their relationship with Jesus is one-sided. It's just based on what they think He can do for them.

People who really love Jesus reach out to Him because they know that He meets their needs. He loves them and takes care of them.

LIVING IT

Luke wants to be a starter on his soccer team. He wants it a lot. But, he doesn't want it enough to work for it. He wants it to happen just like that. He lays on his bed playing video games instead of going to practice and then he prays that God will help him become a starter. Yeah, it doesn't work that way.

Jesus does answer prayer and He does want to help Luke. He might even do a miracle for Luke someday – but not when Luke isn't doing his part!

March 6

> "Come to Me, all you who are weary and burdened and I will give you rest."
> Matthew 11:28

Jesus knows that your life will not always be easy. He didn't promise to make life easy by taking away your problems.

What He did promise is that He will go through the hard times with you. You are not alone. You can lean on Him.

Doesn't it feel good to lean against a wall or a chair when you are really tired? He will help you rest and then give you the strength to keep on going.

The best way to get relief from being tired is to stay close to Jesus.

LIVING IT

George knows about stress! It seems like he always has something to do or something to worry about. He's got school, sports, church, family stuff! Even a kid has a lot to do every day. Add to that any stresses like parents who fight, friends who get mad at you, little sister issues ... and yeah, life gets stressful.

What does George do? He comes close to Jesus. Yep, he closes the door of his room and is just alone with Jesus. He tells Him what is going on and just lets Jesus encourage him and love him.

REMEMBER!

> "This is My body given for you; do this in remembrance of Me."
>
> Luke 22:19

Jesus gave this instruction to His disciples at the Last Supper – the meal they shared with Him before He was arrested.

He told them that from then on when they ate the bread and drank the wine they should remember Him.

He didn't mean they should just remember their friend named Jesus. He meant they should remember what He did for them (and us) by His death and resurrection. He gave the most amazing gift of love.

LIVING IT

Chocolate chip cookies always remind Terry of his grandma. She made the best chocolate chip cookies ever! She died a while ago and Terry misses her. But the cookies always bring the memory of how much fun she was and how much she loved him. That's what the communion service at church is, too. When Terry takes the bread and the grape juice, he remembers Jesus' gift of dying for his sins and coming back to life. It is also a reminder that he will be with Him in heaven someday. It's a connecting time of thankfulness for Terry.

March 8

WHOLE-HEART SERVICE

> "No one can serve two masters. Either he will hate the one and love the other, or he will be devoted to the one and despise the other. You cannot serve both God and Money."
>
> Matthew 6:24

Following God half-heartedly is the same thing as not following God at all. If He doesn't have all the devotion of your heart, then whatever is claiming the other part of it will eventually push God out of the way.

God is not pushy. He waits for you to give all your heart to Him.

For a lot of people money becomes their passion – getting more and more of it. There's nothing wrong with money unless you think more about getting money than you do about God.

LIVING IT

Ken knows that his parents put God first in everything. They give generously of their money when there is any special need around the world and even when there aren't special things, they give. Their money belongs to God, not them. Ken sees others who say they love God, but who spend a lot of time working to make more and more money. They may give some away but not very much. Sure, they have really nice stuff, but do they love and serve God? Doesn't look like it. They have two masters which really means they have one master and it is not God.

March 9

REAL BELIEF

> "Everything is possible for him who believes."
> Mark 9:23

Jesus spoke these words to a father who asked Him to help his son who was demon-possessed.

He just wanted his son to be normal and healthy and happy, and he believed that Jesus could make that happen. Jesus made it sound so simple – just believe and anything is possible.

It isn't simple really, but it is true. The father asked Jesus to help him believe more. He knew his faith wasn't strong enough, but that Jesus could help it grow!

LIVING IT

Brock wants to believe just as this verse says. His mom is very sick and Brock prayed that God would heal her. It hasn't happened yet but Brock knows that God could heal her, if it is His will. He knows that sometimes God doesn't do the things we ask, but he keeps praying because he truly believes God loves him and his mom. Brock asks God to help him believe more and more. The good thing is that Brock knows that Jesus loves his mom even more than he does. He believes God will do what is best for all of them.

Jesus often taught by telling stories. After all, who doesn't enjoy a good story? Here He had just told the story of the Good Samaritan.

> "Go and do likewise."
> Luke 10:37

You know the story: an innocent man is beaten up by robbers. Two different men pass by the poor guy who is lying on the roadside bleeding. They are church men, but they don't help the victim. A third man passes by, a man from Samaria. Although the Samaritans and Jews were enemies, this Good Samaritan stops to help the hurt man.

Jesus finished the story by asking which of the three men was a neighbor to the hurt man. When they answered that it was the third man, Jesus said, "Be like him!"

LIVING IT

Carl has a great example of the special friendship the Good Samaritan showed – his dad! Carl's dad is kind and helpful to everyone he meets. He even goes out of his way to help people who aren't really friends of his, even some who could be considered enemies because they aren't nice to him.

Carl watches his dad be kind and helpful to people who don't return that kindness and he never says a bad word about them. Carl decided, "I want to be like Dad." That's exactly what Jesus suggested – follow a leader who is following Jesus.

GOD KNOWS AND CARES

"Even the very hairs of your head are all numbered. So don't be afraid; you are worth more than many sparrows."
Matthew 10:30-31

Jesus knows everything about you. He knows everything that happens to you. Absolutely nothing surprises Him.

How does that make you feel? Look around you and see the birds flying around. God makes sure they have food and water. He takes care of them.

You matter much more to Him than those birds. He even knows how many hairs there are on your head!

Every detail of your life is known to Him and He cares about them all!

LIVING IT

John wonders if God really cares because some days he and his mom don't have enough food to eat. His mom lost her job and hasn't been able to pay the rent or afford many groceries. Now they might even lose their home. Life looks pretty scary. John tries to pray, but it feels as though God isn't paying attention to their problems. He is though. Deep down inside,

John knows He is and he is learning to trust Him to take care of them ... whatever happens. John knows that he and his mom really do matter to God.

"Others, like seed sown on rocky places, hear the word and at once receive it with joy. But since they have no root, they last only a short time. When trouble or persecution comes because of the word, they quickly fall away."

Mark 4:16-17

Jesus explained how some people receive the news of God's love by comparing it to the way seeds take root in certain kinds of soil.

Some people hear the news of God's love and get excited about it. But they don't read their Bibles and pray so that they can learn to trust God and grow stronger in faith. Then, when problems come they don't have enough faith to keep trusting God.

LIVING IT

Steven is a brand-new Christian. When he's with his Christian friends he is excited and enthusiastic about his new faith. But Steven doesn't read his Bible much or pray very often.

So, when one of his old friends starts giving him a hard time about believing in God, he quickly turns away from God; denies he even knows God; and goes back to hanging out with his non-Christian friends. The roots of Steven's faith are too shallow to keep him strong.

March 13

DOING GOOD

"And if you do good to those who are good to you, what credit is that to you? Even 'sinners' do that."
Luke 6:33

Helping only people who help you is nothing to brag about.

News flash: Just being nice to those who are nice to you is not really obeying Jesus. Yeah, anyone can do that; even if he doesn't know Jesus.

Real evidence that a guy wants to serve Jesus is when he can serve people (not just his friends) and love them. But this doesn't happen without God's help. Loving ALL people, not just your friends, is the goal Jesus has for you!

LIVING IT

You help your friend with his math homework because you're good at it and he isn't. Or, maybe you do your brother's chores because he is super busy. Great! You're helping your friends or family members. But, what if a guy who's been mean to you needs to have his homework delivered when he is out of school sick. Would you volunteer to do it? If you obey Jesus, you will. Anyone can be nice to those who are nice to him. But being nice to your enemies is done because Jesus' love is flowing through you!

March 14

"Everyone who drinks this water will be thirsty again, but whoever drinks the water I give him will never thirst. Indeed, the water I give him will become in him a spring of water welling up to eternal life."

John 4:13-14

What makes you feel really happy? Everyone wants to be happy. People look for happiness in different places. Some want to be leaders. Some work to be the best student in their class. Some hope to be a famous singer or athlete or writer. Whatever it is, people look for satisfaction everywhere except from Jesus.

He says that whatever happiness they find won't last if they don't get their satisfaction from knowing and loving Him. His love is what lasts forever.

LIVING IT

March 15

Patrick wants to be a leader. He dreams of having a group of guys who follow him around and do whatever he says is cool to do. He hopes for guys who hang on his every word. Patrick wants this more than anything. He believes that would truly make him happy.

He's wrong. Patrick doesn't realize that he would be working all the time to stay at the top of the group. Yeah, what Patrick hasn't realized is that the only thing that will really make him happy is to accept Jesus and put all his energy into serving Him.

BY THE BOOK

> "Let it be so now; it is proper for us to do this to fulfill all righteousness."
>
> Matthew 3:15

Jesus said this to John the Baptist. He had just asked John to baptize him and John tried to stop Him.

John said that Jesus should be baptizing him instead. But, Jesus always paid close attention to what was right.

He didn't want anyone to be able to say that He wasn't truly the Messiah because things didn't happen the way the prophets had said they would. He wanted to do things by the book.

Think about it ... If Jesus lived by the book (the Bible) then so should we.

LIVING IT

Luca knew all the right things to say. He could pray out loud using fancy words that made him sound really smart and very serious about following God.

Weird thing though ... Luca had never actually asked Jesus to be his Savior. He was banking on the fact that his parents were Christians. He thought he could get into heaven by just going with them. Luca had to learn that there are no shortcuts to serving God. He had to accept Jesus himself and do things "by the book." Just like Jesus did!

March 16

STICK CLOSE TO JESUS!

"I have told you these things, so that in Me you may have peace. In this world you will have trouble. But take heart! I have overcome the world."
John 16:33

This world is full of all kinds of troubles. Jesus was speaking to His disciples when He said these words. He knows that even people who follow Him will have trouble.

Sometimes the troubles come just because you follow Him. People in the world don't get why you would follow and obey Jesus.

He promised to give peace to those who follow Him. He promised that He would be with you. And, He reminds you that no matter what kind of troubles the world throws at you ... He will win!

LIVING IT

Craig recently became a Christian. Not many of his friends are Christians so this is a new thing for him ... and all of them. Craig knows that becoming a Christian does not mean he will have no more problems. But, he didn't expect that some of his old friends would get really angry about his new faith.

Craig is thankful for this verse that reminds him that Jesus is stronger than anyone who is against him. He believes he will get through tough times by staying close to Jesus!

REAL TRUTH

"All the nations will be gathered before Him, and He will separate the people one from another as a shepherd separates the sheep from the goats."
Matthew 25:32

One day in the future every person will stand before God. Each person will have to answer for his choice of whether or not to accept Jesus as Savior.

People who have spent their lives only pretending to be Christians when it was convenient will find out that they did not fool God.

He will separate the believers from the unbelievers. The believers will come to heaven to be with Him. He looks at people's hearts and sees the truth.

LIVING IT

Charley is a great actor. He has fooled everyone into thinking he has a strong faith in Jesus. Yep, he knows all the right things to say and do. He even does good things like helping others and volunteering for missions trips. These are all good things to do, but Jesus isn't his motivation.

Sure, Charley can fool lots of people – but he can't fool God. He sees Charley's heart and knows he has not asked Jesus to be his Savior. Charley can't be a part of God's family by pretending. It has to be real.

March 18

> "Why do you entertain evil thoughts in your hearts?"
> Matthew 9:4

What does "entertaining evil thoughts in your heart" mean? It means you think about doing things that you know are not things God wants you to do.

Jesus knew that sometimes people choose to think evil thoughts that pull them away from God. Evil thoughts can lead to questioning God, even about His love for you.

The Bible tells us to guard our hearts because Satan gets into our lives through hearts that aren't guarded.

Keep your heart focused on God, His love for you and the truths of the Bible. Then there is no room for evil thoughts.

LIVING IT

Questions are not bad. Asking questions and looking for answers or learning from mature Christians helps your faith to grow. It's OK to ask questions because you will never understand everything about God or about the Christian life. But, entertaining evil thoughts is like what Brandon did when he started thinking about doing things that he knew God would not approve of. Brandon spent a lot of time thinking about how he would do these things and what it would feel like. When Brandon had those kinds of thoughts, his heart was focused on evil things and not on God's love and care.

March 19

MERCY IS AS MERCY DOES

> "Be merciful, just as your Father is merciful."
> Luke 6:36

God treats each of His children with mercy. He is kind and forgiving toward them.

Jesus told us to treat others that way, too. We receive kindness and forgiveness from God, even when we do not deserve it.

Since we have been treated so kindly, Jesus says we should treat others in the same way. Our Father (isn't it cool to know that God is our Father?) wants us to do so.

LIVING IT

Sam gets along with just about everybody. The one person he has trouble with is his little brother, Casey. He is such a pain! When Sam's friends come over to play, Casey keeps butting in. They can't even play a board game without him wrecking everything. Sam gets so angry but then he remembers how God is always merciful and forgiving to him and that Casey just wants to be a big boy like his super cool brother. So, Sam forgives Casey and offers mercy to him – just as God does to Sam!

March 20

> "Take care of
> My sheep."
> John 21:16

Peter was a super close friend with Jesus. One time, Peter told some people that he didn't even know Jesus. Later Jesus wanted to know how Peter really felt about Him so He asked Peter three times if he really loved Him. Of course Peter answered yes each time.

After each answer, Jesus told him something to do – this time it was, "feed My sheep."

Loving Jesus is more than just saying words; when you love Him, you serve Him and that means action.

LIVING IT

Chase wants to put his love for Jesus into action but he just isn't sure what he can do. After all, he's only 10 years old. So, he gathers a couple of his friends and they come up with a plan.

They form a team who looks for ways to help neighbors and people from their church with yard work, errands or anything else they can find to do. They look for ways to take care of Jesus' sheep!

FOR OR AGAINST HIM

"He who is not with Me is against Me, and he who does not gather with Me scatters."
Matthew 12:30

Maybe you've heard the old saying, "Not to decide is to decide." That's what Jesus is saying with this statement.

Once a person has heard about Jesus' love, then he either chooses Jesus or he doesn't. Yeah, it's his responsibility to choose to accept Jesus or not. He can't say, "Oh, I'll decide later" because that is actually deciding not to accept Him.

So, if you aren't for Jesus then you are against Him ... not a good place to be.

LIVING IT

What does it look like to be against Jesus? Well, a person who is against Him would try to keep others away from Him. He would do whatever he could to keep others from believing in Jesus or trusting His word. He would not be loving, kind and merciful to others. He would be pretty much the opposite of everything Jesus is.

On the other hand, being "with Jesus" means that Jesus lives in his heart and guides his thoughts and actions in ways that honor Him and pull others closer to Him.

> "Whoever does God's will is My brother and sister and mother."
>
> Mark 3:35

Don't you just love your family? Why are family relationships so cool? Family members can be themselves with one another. They love one another totally (even if they don't always like one another).

Being a member of God's family is the best thing ever. It's only possible because Jesus, God's Son, came to earth, lived and died for our sins and then rose again to life.

He said that anyone can be a member of His family by doing God's will, which means obeying Him and loving Him.

LIVING IT

Ryan has a super cool family. He has awesome parents, an older sister and younger brother. He has good friends, too, but really enjoys his family. That helps him understand the privilege of being a member of God's family. It's the closest relationship he can have with God.

He understands "doing God's will" to mean that he obeys God, which begins with reading His Word so he knows what to obey. It means serving Him by loving Him and loving others. Doing God's will is living a life of love.

"PROVE IT" PRAYERS

In the middle of Satan trying to get Jesus to turn away from God, Jesus quoted this verse from the Old Testament.

Why is this important? Because it proved that Jesus knew the Scriptures. Think about it – if Scripture was important enough for Jesus to know, then we should know them, too.

It's also important because it says that we shouldn't test God's love for us by saying, "If You love me You will do ... whatever." God **does** love us and He does what is best for us. He proves it every day.

LIVING IT

"OK God, if You really do love me like You say You do, then let me pass my English final," Zeke prayed. "If I pass then I'll **know** that You love me," he prayed.

Yeah, putting God to the test is not such a good idea. He doesn't answer Your prayers even to prove something. He does what is best for you and shows you every day that He loves you. Don't do "prove it" kinds of prayers. Just trust Him.

> "Now that I, your Lord and Teacher, have washed your feet, you also should wash one another's feet."
> John 13:14

Imagine having your feet washed by the Son of God. It would be pretty humbling, right?

Jesus did wash His disciples' feet even though that's a job usually done by servants. He did it to give a beautiful example of a servant's heart that serves others in basic, simple and unglamorous ways.

A servant's heart serves out of love. Jesus told His disciples (and us) that we should do the same.

LIVING IT

When the church van pulled into the parking lot after a long, hot day at the amusement park all the kids piled out and left. The youth pastor and other adults looked tiredly at the candy wrappers, water bottles and other assorted trash left in the van.

Then they heard a single voice say, "I'll clean it up while you make sure all the parents are here." Tommy, one of the youngest guys in the group volunteered to serve them and really serve the entire group by cleaning out the van. He served them, just as Jesus served His disciples by washing their feet. Love in action!

THE POWER OF PRAYER

> "If you believe, you will receive whatever you ask for in prayer."
> Matthew 21:22

Jesus wanted His followers to believe in Him and understand His amazing power. He wanted them to trust Him completely.

Does that sound a little unbelievable – like if you did that you could get whatever you want from God? That makes Him sound like a big Santa Claus, doesn't it?

But, it isn't that simple. When you believe in Jesus, read the Bible and try to obey God, then you end up wanting what He wants for you instead of what you might want for yourself. And you accept His answers to your prayers because you believe He knows what is best for you.

LIVING IT

Pete used to want to be the best baseball player in the whole world. He practiced hours every day so that he could make that happen. He even prayed that God would make him the best baseball player ever. But, when Pete gave his life to Jesus, he began to trust God to guide his life, even if it meant no baseball.

Now Pete spends time reading God's Word and learning to serve Him, so the "wants" he prays for now have changed to things that God actually wants to give him! Pete's desires will begin to match God's!

March 26

STAY FOCUSED

Jesus replied, "No one who puts his hand to the plow and looks back is fit for service in the kingdom of God."
Luke 9:62

Each of Jesus' followers has important work to do. Jesus knows that sometimes the job you have to do requires staying focused.

It isn't possible to do the work well if you are looking around at other people or other things and comparing yourself to them.

Just as a farmer has to watch where he's going if he is going to plow a straight line, God's worker needs to pay attention to the work he is doing and where he is going.

LIVING IT

"Matt, will you please weed the garden for me?" Mom asked. But, Matt didn't want to do that job. So he pulled a few weeds then lay back on the lawn and watched the clouds floating by.

Mark didn't stay focused on his job – that's what Jesus is talking about in this verse – looking around at other things instead of paying attention to the work you should be doing. This is especially important when doing a job God gives you to do – pay attention and do it well!

March 27

FOLLOW THE LEADER

"Come, follow Me," Jesus said, "and I will make you fishers of men."
Mark 1:17

Before Jesus called them to follow Him, several of the men Jesus called to be His disciples were fishermen.

When He asked each of them to follow Him, He explained what their new jobs would be – fishing for people. Kind of a weird thing to say, huh?

But, He was calling them to the job of telling people about God's love and to encourage people to believe that Jesus was the Son of God. Pretty cool job!

LIVING IT

Trey loves to go fishing with his grandpa. He has learned that fishing takes a lot of patience and that sometimes he has to be quiet so that the fish would come close. Actual fishing is a good model for what needs to happen to "fish" for people to accept Christ.

Trey gets it – fishing for people to accept Christ as Savior takes patience, and sometimes being quiet and listening to people. He is sure he can do it! It's the job Jesus gives him to do!

> Jesus answered, "It is written: 'Man does not live on bread alone, but on every word that comes from the mouth of God.'"
>
> Matthew 4:4

During Jesus' time on earth, some people fasted (went without food) for a few days at a time to show how spiritual they were.

They weren't really that connected to God; they were actually just trying to show off. If they were truly fasting to honor God, they would spend the time praying and seeking His guidance.

Jesus blew their cover by saying that whether they fasted or ate was not the important thing – knowing and obeying God's Word is what really matters.

Show-offs are just show-offs. Loving God comes from the heart.

LIVING IT

Henry brags about all the good stuff he does. He wants to make sure that everyone knows when he helps another person. He quotes Bible verses and sings Christian choruses. Henry thinks all this stuff proves that he really loves God.

But, Henry doesn't understand the Bible verses he quotes and he doesn't really care about others. Henry is all show and no real action. Loving God comes from the heart. Bragging means nothing – knowing God's Word and obeying Him is what really matters.

March 29

BORN AGAIN

> "You should not
> be surprised
> at My saying,
> 'You must be
> born again.'"
>
> John 3:7

A man asked Jesus some questions about who Jesus was and why He was able to do such amazing miracles.

Jesus had a simple answer as to what would help this man understand His work. He said, "You must be born again."

Being born again is not referring to a physical kind of birth, but a birth of the heart. You are born again when you ask Jesus to come into your heart. He does that through the power of the Holy Spirit and then you are born into His family and everything God does and the words of the Bible make sense to you.

LIVING IT

Erik goes to Sunday school and church every week. But, not because he really "gets" the whole God thing. He goes because he has friends there and usually there are fun things going on.

But, when the teacher starts the lesson or the minister begins his sermon, Erik tunes out. None of it makes any sense to him. It won't make sense until the day he asks Jesus to forgive his sins and be his Savior – when he is born again!

March 30

OPENED EYES

> "Open your eyes and look at the fields! They are ripe for harvest."
> John 4:35

Jesus' disciples didn't always understand why He took the time to stop and talk with some people.

The harvest He mentions in this verse is not crops; it is people. He wanted all people to know God. That was His harvest.

The disciples needed to stop looking at things from a human viewpoint such as, "Why does Jesus take time to talk with people who are not important?" Their eyes needed to be opened to God's viewpoint that all people need to know God!

LIVING IT

When Jamie read these words of Jesus he prayed for God to open his eyes. God pointed him to Paul. Paul was not cool at all. He wasn't good at sports or music and not especially smart. Most kids made fun of him – even to his face. They really picked on him and even bullied him.

The thing is, none of them took the time to get to know Paul. God helped Jamie see Paul as a person who needed to know God's love. So, Jamie spent time with Paul and soon they became friends and then Jamie could share God's love with his friend.

March 31

GOOD HUNGER

> "Blessed are those who hunger and thirst for righteousness, for they will be filled."
>
> Matthew 5:6

What do you dream for your own future? Everyone hungers for something. Some people want fame or power. Some want lots of money. Some want success. Some just want to win at whatever they are doing and they are quick to criticize anyone who isn't a winner by their standards.

Most people hunger for things they don't have. Jesus' words here are a challenge to hunger and thirst for God – for the purpose of pleasing Him and serving Him and seeing His will done in your life.

If that's what you want, you will have your desires granted.

LIVING IT

Brian has friends who dream of being world-class athletes. Others dream of being leaders in their country. Big goals. Brian's dream is to help people around the world to have better lives. God planted that dream in Brian's heart.

So, while his friends are practicing and studying to make their goals come true, Brian's focus is for all people to be treated fairly and for all people to have food and water. More than anything, he longs for all the people of earth to have the opportunity to know God's love. Yes, you could say that he hungered for that!

April 1

US AGAINST THEM

In Jesus' day an attitude developed of "us against them." That attitude is still around today. Big surprise, huh? People are divided by what they believe or by what they like.

Guys hang around with people who like what they like and think the way they think. They sometimes are not very nice toward anyone who is different. Jesus' response to that behavior was, "Stop it." You should love your enemies as much as you love your friends. God does and blesses all people, not just the ones who agree with you.

> "You have heard that it was said, 'Love your neighbor and hate your enemy.' But I tell you: Love your enemies and pray for those who persecute you, that you may be sons of your Father in heaven. He causes His sun to rise on the evil and the good, and sends rain on the righteous and the unrighteous."
>
> Matthew 5:43-45

LIVING IT

Mike and Steven are both going for first-chair violin in their school orchestra. The competition is tough because they both play well. The sad thing is that the competition got ugly. There was name-calling and nasty tricks. By the time the orchestra director was ready to choose the orchestra had divided into the Mike team and the Steven team. Mike was awarded first-chair and Steven was hurt and angry but then he remembered what Jesus taught. He went to Mike and congratulated him and calmed the ugly battle.

April 2

GROW UP!

> "Be perfect, therefore, as your heavenly Father is perfect."
> Matthew 5:48

Perfect? Was Jesus kidding? No one is perfect except Him, right?

Well, the Greek word Jesus used for perfection means something more like maturity. So, actually Jesus was saying, "Grow up. Act your age."

He said this in the middle of the Sermon on the Mount, where He gave a lot of instruction on how to live for God and how to treat others. So, He's saying, "Put what I've taught you to practice in your life. Live maturely."

LIVING IT

Eric was irritated with his little brother. "Get out of my room!" he screamed at Ty who actually looked scared as he ran down the hall, right past Mom. Eric slammed his bedroom door and dropped down on the floor by his bed. He knew what was coming. The door opened and Mom said, "Eric, you're 5 years older than Ty. I know brothers can be a pain sometimes – I have one, too. But, you should be able to behave more maturely. You're a Christian and you know what Jesus taught about loving others and living His way. Do you think you just did that?" Eric gulped. "No, I'll apologize to Ty. I'm sorry, Mom."

April 3

ALL ABOUT GOD

People have often wondered why bad things happen to good people. Some think the bad things that happen are punishment for sin.

That's what the men talking to Jesus suggested about a man who was born blind. They thought that his blindness was punishment for his parents' sin. But, Jesus turned their thoughts to another direction.

Sometimes bad things just happen. What's important is that God is glorified – either by taking away the bad thing or by the person's trust in Him during the hard time. It's all about God; not people.

> "Neither this man nor his parents sinned," said Jesus, "but this happened so that the work of God might be displayed in his life."
>
> John 9:3

LIVING IT

Mark is scared and worried. His grandpa is really sick and Mark is worried that ... well ... that he might not get well. He prays for grandpa all the time, asking God to make him well again.

Mark wants to go fishing with him and do woodworking projects like they used to do. Mark does know that Grandpa loves God and trusts Him to take care of him. So, Mark knows that Grandpa believes the most important thing is for God to be glorified – whatever happens.

April 4

> Then He said to them all: "If anyone would come after Me, he must deny himself and take up his cross daily and follow Me."
> Luke 9:23

This is Jesus' plain and simple definition of what it means to follow Him.

You've got to be all the way in or you're not in at all. Being a follower of Jesus means life is all about Him – loving Him, obeying Him, living for Him, learning more about Him.

A true disciple cannot hold back a part of his life – such as what sites he visits on the internet, or how he treats others.

Life is all about following Jesus.

LIVING IT

Nick has a secret. It's a secret because no one knows about it – it's in his thoughts. Nick lets his mind wander to think about things that he knows would not make Jesus proud of him. Nick thinks that if no one knows about his thoughts then it can't affect their opinions of his Christianity.

But what Nick forgets is that Jesus knows. There are no secrets from Him. He knows that Nick isn't all the way in to following Him because he is holding this one part of his thoughts back. Following Jesus means getting all the way in!

April 5

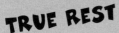

TRUE REST

> "Take My yoke upon you and learn from Me, for I am gentle and humble in heart, and you will find rest for your souls."
>
> Matthew 11:29

Jesus knows that life is sometimes stressful. You can get buried under a load of schoolwork. Family problems can be so hard. Tensions in your friendships are exhausting.

Yeah, there is a lot for you to deal with every day. Jesus knows that but it isn't hopeless.

He offers a solution – Himself. His strength and gentleness will get you through whatever problems you face. Rest in Him.

LIVING IT

Denny heard a fist smash against a wall. His dad was yelling again. It seemed like he was always angry these days. Denny covered his head with a pillow. "I can't take this anymore. I want to run away. Make him stop!" he prayed.

As Denny lay in the darkness, he prayed again, "Help me, Jesus. Help me." Suddenly a feeling of peace floated over him like a soft blanket. Jesus answered that prayer and Denny found rest and peace in Him.

April 6

FORGIVEN

> "Therefore, I tell you, her many sins have been forgiven – for she loved much. But he who has been forgiven little loves little."
>
> Luke 7:47

A man who thought he had lived a pretty good life came to talk to Jesus. This man didn't think he needed much forgiveness because he didn't think he had sinned much.

Then Jesus spoke of a woman who had lived a pretty sinful life. She knew that she had been forgiven for a lot so she worshiped Jesus with all her heart.

Understanding how much Jesus has done for you makes you love Him even more!

LIVING IT

Cade thinks he has life figured out and has very few problems. Cade has accepted Jesus, but doesn't really think about Him much because he doesn't really see why he needs to. He doesn't think he needs Jesus' help with life.

Josh, on the other hand, has allowed Jesus to soften his heart and make him aware of the times he falls short in his effort to live for Him. Josh asks Jesus' forgiveness often and knows that He gives it. Josh loves Jesus with all His heart and is so thankful for His grace and forgiveness.

Which boy has it right?

BLIND LEADERSHIP!

> "If a blind man leads a blind man, both will fall into a pit."
> Matthew 15:14

The Pharisees were the religious leaders of Jesus' time. They thought they knew everything. But they didn't.

They were living by rules they made up, not by God's commands. Not only that, they tried to insist that everyone follow their rules. They were a perfect example of the blind leading the blind.

Jesus warned His followers about following the Pharisees' rules and thinking they were obeying God by doing so. They weren't.

LIVING IT

For some reason Zach had a lot of power over other guys. They followed him and did whatever he said was the cool thing to do. John was one of Zach's followers. But he was uncomfortable with some of the things Zach led the guys to do. Some of the things were mean and dishonest. Sure, it was fun and they got good laughs out of it. But, sometimes other people got hurt. John's eyes were being opened to the dangers of following someone who wasn't leading in a good way. John decided to turn away from Zach's leadership.

April 8

> "The things that come out of the mouth come from the heart, and these make a man 'unclean.'"
>
> Matthew 15:18

Words have so much power! Maybe you can remember a time when someone said something mean to you. It took a long time to get over it, didn't it? (If you have yet).

Jesus said the words that fly out of our mouths show what kind of stuff is going on in our hearts. If you're selfish, mean-spirited and prideful then all that stuff will show by the words you speak to others.

Clean up your heart and your words will clean up, too.

LIVING IT

April 9

Vince is really funny and often says things that make his buddies laugh. But the problem is that some of Vince's funniest stuff is when he is "teasing" other guys. He's really making fun of them but makes it sound like a joke.

Vince's comments hurt those guys, and actually show what his true opinion of them is. He can tell them that he's joking, but the truth is that his jokes show what an unkind, selfish heart Vince has.

PERSONAL CHOICE

> "But what about you?" He asked. "Who do you say I am?"
> Matthew 16:15

Peter was one of Jesus' closest friends. Sometimes Peter spouted words before he thought, but there was no doubt that he loved Jesus.

In this conversation Jesus asks Peter if people are saying that He truly is God's Son.

After Peter answered that question Jesus asked this one, "What about you, Peter? Who do you say I am?"

You see, faith in Jesus is a personal decision. You don't become a Christian just because your parents are or just because you hang out with church kids. It's your own choice and you must accept Jesus personally.

LIVING IT

Evan's parents are devoted Christians and their faith means a lot to them. They have family devotional time every day where they read from the Bible and pray together. They love God and serve Him enthusiastically. Since Evan has grown up with Christianity being a part of every day, he just assumes he's a Christian, too. But, it doesn't work that way.

Evan needs to confess that Jesus is God's Son who died for his sins and rose again. He must ask Jesus to be his Savior, personally.

April '10

JESUS FREAK!

> "If the world hates you, keep in mind that it hated Me first."
> John 15:18

Jesus wasn't popular with some people. The ones who hated Him the most were actually the religious leaders, weird, huh?

They didn't like that He taught different things than they did. They didn't like that He didn't keep all the rules they had made up. Since they hated Jesus, it only makes sense that they hated His followers, too.

That still happens sometimes today. People who are against God will be against His followers. That's OK, just keep on doing what God wants you to do. He will take care of you.

LIVING IT

Chuck makes no secret of the fact that he is a Christian. He doesn't try to hide that he goes to church. He says a quick prayer before he eats lunch. He doesn't really care what the other kids think. And some of them think a lot. A couple of guys who don't care about God at all have twisted Chuck's name to be "Church." They give him a hard time about being a God-boy.

But Chuck is OK with it. He doesn't get mad. He doesn't try to get even. He just keeps right on living for God and will let God deal with the guys.

TOO PROUD TO LOVE

> "Everyone who exalts himself will be humbled, and he who humbles himself will be exalted."
>
> Luke 18:14

Jesus never had any good to say about people who toot their own horns or braggers.

Some people think so much of themselves that they feel they are more important than other people and entitled to be treated better; to get what they want and to be first all the time.

There is absolutely nothing about that behavior that says love and God is all about love. People like that will answer to Jesus because of their inflated view of themselves.

LIVING IT

Dallas is a nice guy but he has a slight learning disability and a little trouble speaking. Most of the guys are friendly to him and he has a couple of good friends. But one guy, Adam, thinks he is way better than Dallas. He usually just ignores Dallas, but if Dallas should happen to get in his way Adam is pretty unkind.

He says things that are mean and sometimes even pushes Dallas out of the way. Adam thinks he is pretty important and shouldn't have to deal with Dallas. He is not showing love to Dallas and he will have to explain his actions to Jesus someday!

April 12

"Everyone who does evil hates the light, and will not come into the light for fear that his deeds will be exposed."

John 3:20

What specific light is Jesus referring to in this statement? Himself!

Earlier He said, "I am the light of the world." Now He is just pointing out that people who enjoy doing their wicked things will stay away from Him because otherwise they have to face their own sinfulness.

It's easier to deny that you are a sinner if you think no one knows what you do. But, when you stand near Jesus (the light) everything is revealed.

LIVING IT

Bullies are classic examples of staying away from the light. They get away with pushing other kids around and saying rotten things as long as no one stands up to them.

But, when a bully is confronted with the truth and passion of Jesus' love, all their ugliness is revealed, even to their own hearts, and they have to change. They can't stay near Jesus and continue behaving that way.

April 13

FOOD AND WATER

Grapes grow on vines. The smaller branches of the grapevine get their food and water from the vine itself.

Without that connection the branches will starve and there will be no grapes.

Jesus is the vine of life for His people. Staying connected to Him through prayer and reading your Bible is how you get nourishment. Without Jesus you can't really do anything.

LIVING IT

Grandpa gave Mark a seedling – a tiny little sprout of a tree. He told him to plant it in the back yard when he got home and give it lots of water so it could grow. Mark forgot all about it when he got home and the seedling lay in the car for several days. When he finally did remember it Mark ran to get it but the seedling was shriveled and dried up. What happened? The seedling was cut off from all sources of nutrition. Its roots couldn't get water. So it died – much like a Christian who doesn't stay close to Jesus to get the nutrition to make him grow.

April 14

> "Go, sell everything you have and give to the poor, and you will have treasure in heaven. Then come, follow Me."
> Mark 10:21

A rich man came to Jesus and asked how he could have eternal life. Jesus' answer was the same as He always taught – love and care for others.

The foundation of a life with Jesus is loving others. Jesus told him to sell the stuff he owned and use the money to help other people. That would show his unselfishness and care for others. That would give him treasure in heaven.

Sadly, the rich man would not do it, would you?

LIVING IT

Alex has lots of stuff – cool games, a laptop, a music system. He gets pretty much anything he wants. Alex heard about some kids who lost everything they had (which really wasn't much to begin with) because an earthquake wrecked their homes.

It would have been nice if Alex was touched enough to want to share what he had with those kids. But, he wasn't. Alex hadn't allowed his heart to be touched with Jesus' love for others. He could not love the way Jesus loves.

April 15

NO TESTING ALLOWED

> "It is also written: 'Do not put the Lord your God to the test.'"
>
> Matthew 4:7

Satan was tempting Jesus. He was trying to get Jesus to turn away from God and worship him. Satan offered some pretty cool things to try to tempt Jesus, but none of them worked.

Jesus refused every temptation by quoting Scripture. So one of Satan's temptations was to challenge Scripture – make Jesus prove that God would do what He says He will do.

Jesus answered with this verse – don't try to test God. He doesn't have to prove anything to you.

LIVING IT

Is it a big temptation to test God to prove His love for you? Do you ever secretly pray, "God, if You really love me then do this or that?" Your prayer ends up being a test that God must pass to prove Himself to you. If you feel the need to put God to the test it may mean that you don't really trust Him or His love for you. It's hard sometimes not to give in to this temptation because you may just want to "feel" His love. But, instead of testing Him, just remember all He has done for you and all the ways He shows you His love.

"You are the light of the world. A city on a hill cannot be hidden."

Matthew 5:14

Jesus called Himself the Light of the World so it only makes sense that His followers are also light in a dark world.

The world is dark because of sin – the selfish, mean and bad things that people do. The light that comes from Jesus' love and righteousness shows the bad things in your life.

Jesus tells His followers that because they follow Him they shine His light into a dark world. They should never try to hide that light because it leads to God and His love.

LIVING IT

Rob is tempted to just keep quiet about the fact that he is a Christian. Some of the guys he knows make fun of him for talking about God.

But, he has noticed that when he is around those same guys are a bit more careful about the language they use or the things they say. Rob knows that it's because he is shining Jesus' light into a dark world. How cool is that?

April 17

WATCH YOUR WORDS

The words that come out of your mouth say a lot about what thoughts are racing through your mind. Believe it or not, they also reveal your opinion of who Jesus is.

These words of Jesus are right in the middle of His famous Sermon on the Mount; in which He gave many instructions on how to live in ways that honor God.

The bottom line here is be careful what you say. It says a lot about you.

"I tell you, do not swear at all: either by heaven, for it is God's throne; or by the earth, for it is His footstool; or by Jerusalem, for it is the city of the Great King. And do not swear by your head, for you cannot make even one hair white or black. Simply let your 'Yes' be 'Yes,' and your 'No,' 'No'; anything beyond this comes from the evil one."

Matthew 5:34-37

LIVING IT

Max has friends who are so much fun to be with! They make him laugh and they think of awesome things to do. The problem is that some of them use words that Max's parents have forbidden him to use. They use God's name like a swear word and they use slang words that are not very nice.

Max has to be careful not to pick up their habits. He doesn't want them to think he's weird but he also doesn't want to offend God by the way he speaks.

April 18

PRIVATE PRAYER

"When you pray, go into your room, close the door and pray to your Father, who is unseen. Then your Father, who sees what is done in secret, will reward you."

Matthew 6:6

Prayer is a very personal conversation. Much like when you have a private chat with a good friend.

Prayer is between you and God. So keep it private. Jesus' instruction is not to make a big show of praying in public about your personal and private requests.

Keep it between you and God. He will hear and He will answer.

LIVING IT

Some people make a big show of everything they do. They demand a lot of attention. They do the same thing when they pray. They use big, fancy words. Their voices get very dramatic and they pray with lots of emotion. That does not mean that God hears their prayers more than anyone else's.

Jesus said prayer about your personal problems, fears and needs is between you and God. You don't have to make a big show of it. Just pray. Alone. Quietly. Then listen for God's answer.

BABY STEPS

> "Whoever can be trusted with very little can also be trusted with much, and whoever is dishonest with very little will also be dishonest with much."
>
> Luke 16:10

Some guys want to be important and influential. However, according to Jesus, no one gets big responsibilities before proving himself able to handle small ones.

Jesus is saying, "Show me I can trust you with small jobs and when you've proven yourself trustworthy and honest, then I'll give you bigger and more important jobs."

So, start small. Prove yourself. Move up.

LIVING IT

"I just want to go to the arcade with my friends. Why won't you let me go?" Brian whined. "You don't trust me!" Dad said, "You're right. We don't. Remember, we gave you some responsibility and freedom a few weeks ago and you didn't handle it well. You broke our simple rules, so now you have to earn our trust again."

Brian didn't say anything – he couldn't. He remembered Jesus' words that proved Dad's point. Be trustworthy in small things and then be trusted with more!

SIMPLE BELIEF

April 21

> "Unless you people see miraculous signs and wonders," Jesus told him, "you will never believe."
>
> John 4:48

It must have made Jesus sad that people wouldn't believe He was God's Son unless He did some big miracle for them.

Why couldn't people love Him because He is God's Son and He loved them first?

It's a human thing that when we are given stuff it makes us feel that we are loved more easily than just hearing or reading, "God loves you."

LIVING IT

"What did you bring me?" Kirk asked. His dad was just home from a business trip and before saying, "I missed you or how was your trip?" Kirk wanted to know what he got. Kirk's question made Dad feel as though Kirk would love him more if he brought him a gift.

Unfortunately, Kirk approached God the same way with a "What will you do for me today?" attitude. Too bad – he missed the basic message of the Bible – God loves you, Kirk!

FOLLOW JESUS

"Follow Me,"
Jesus said.
Luke 5:27

Two simple words. Some kids' games are made up of the idea of following someone and doing what the leader does. It's not a big deal, is it? Nope, except when it is.

The truth is that in real life pretty much everyone follows somebody. Some people think following someone will help them be popular or accepted or considered successful in some way.

Jesus knew that people are followers so He made it simple. Follow Him. That leads to peace and happiness.

LIVING IT

Rob is a follower. He doesn't have enough confidence to feel like a leader so he chose to follow Dan. Dan has lots of friends and he is always thinking of weird things to do.

The problem is that Dan doesn't always make good choices so he gets in trouble and Rob gets in trouble by following him. Rob knows that sometimes Dan leads him away from obeying Jesus. He needs to learn to trust himself enough to follow Jesus and not anyone else.

April 22

> "I ask you, which is lawful on the Sabbath: to do good or to do evil, to save life or to destroy it?"
>
> Luke 6:9

Have you ever wondered if Jesus got tired of the Pharisees nagging Him?

They were great rule-makers and wanted everyone to live by their rules. What got lost in their world of rules was love and concern for other people, something that was very important to Jesus.

He cared about people, not man-made rules.

LIVING IT

Ryan loved his grandfather. He spent time with him whenever he could. Everyone loved Ryan's grandpa. He could fix anything!

He helped his neighbors when their lawnmowers wouldn't run. He shoveled snow for a friend who had a broken arm. He made woodworking projects to give away. Ryan's grandpa cared about people, no matter who they were.

April 23

HEAR, BELIEVE AND LIVE

> "I tell you the truth, whoever hears My word and believes Him who sent Me has eternal life and will not be condemned; he has crossed over from death to life."
>
> John 5:24

Jesus made it clear that there is only one pathway to eternal life.

Many times He encouraged people to learn from His teachings, believe in God's love and accept Him as their Savior. That's the only path to heaven and eternal life.

Some people try to say there is another way but there is not. Only one way ... Jesus.

LIVING IT

Some people look for the easiest way to get things done, even if it means they don't do their best job. Some people cheat to take shortcuts to finish projects. That means they don't do their best work, too.

One thing that there is no shortcut for is the way to get eternal life in heaven. No shortcuts. No way other than trusting Jesus and believing in Him. Chris learned that when he was six years old and has been sharing that good news with his friends ever since. Jesus is the only way!

April 24

> "This son of mine was dead and is alive again; he was lost and is found." So they began to celebrate.
>
> Luke 15:24

Jesus said this as He told the story of the Prodigal Son – a story of a boy who disrespected his father and left home.

The boy spent all the money his father gave him so he was homeless and had nothing to eat. When he decided to go home and ask his father to give him a job, not even to treat him as a son anymore, the father welcomed him home and threw a party to celebrate that his son was home!

That's exactly what happens when a person accepts Jesus as Savior – a party in heaven!

LIVING IT

Will's 18-year-old brother got so mad at Mom and Dad that he left home and no one heard from him for a long time. Will missed him a lot. Then one day he showed up at the front door. Will wondered if Mom and Dad would be angry at him or punish him for all the worry he caused. But, they didn't.

They celebrated that he was home again because they loved him. God's love is the same way – welcoming sinners who accept Jesus as Savior. Parties in heaven, for you!

April 25

NO JUDGING!

The basis of Jesus' teaching is love –
love God and love others.

It's pretty hard to criticize or judge
someone if you're busy loving them. Judging often comes before loving because some
people think everyone else should live by their rules.
When people don't live by those rules, they are judged to
be "not serious Christians" or even "not nice people."

Don't judge others because if you do, Jesus says you
will be judged yourself ... by God.

LIVING IT

What does it mean to judge others? You judge others when
you decide for yourself that another guy is not as smart as you
or not as athletic or not as important.

When you make a judgment about another person you are
being unfair to him. You don't want to be unfairly judged, do
you? Well, don't judge anyone else, because you will be judged
by the same measurement.

April 26

NOT FOR SHOW

"Be careful not to do your 'acts of righteousness' before men, to be seen by them. If you do, you will have no reward from your Father in heaven."

Matthew 6:1

Jesus warned His followers against doing good things just to show off to others. That means don't do good things just so other people will see you do them and then think good things about you.

It doesn't matter what other people think about you. It only matters what Jesus thinks.

He doesn't look at your show-off acts; He looks at your heart to see whether or not you really care about others.

LIVING IT

There's no doubt that Brent did a lot of nice things for other people. He worked with young boys in an after-school program. He ran errands for an older neighbor. Nice things.

The problem is that Brent made sure everyone knew about anything nice he did. He bragged constantly to his friends. So, according to Jesus' words, Brent was getting his reward right now – not when he stands before God in heaven.

KEEP YOUR FOCUS

"Let us go somewhere else – to the nearby villages – so I can preach there also. That is why I have come."
Mark 1:38

Jesus knew why He was on earth. He left heaven to come to earth as a human being because He and God had a plan.

They wanted to have personal relationships with people so that it would be possible for people to know God and one day be in heaven with Him.

Jesus didn't let pressure from other people distract Him from what He came to do. He was focused on His job.

LIVING IT

Sonny is only twelve years old and for about ten of those years he thought that he would be a professional baseball player when he grew up. That was his dream anyway and he practiced every single day to get better at baseball. Then, he asked Jesus into his heart.

Now Sonny wants to use his life to share God's love with others so he reads his Bible and learns all he can about it. He is focused on doing what God wants him to do.

April 28

> "The work of
> God is this:
> to believe in
> the one He
> has sent."
> John 6:29

Some men came to Jesus and asked what they had to do in order to do what God required.

Jesus had a simple answer. He said they just needed to believe in Him. Believe that God sent Jesus and that He is definitely God's Son.

Now, that may sound pretty basic. But, the truth is, if you really believe that Jesus is God's Son then you will want to know Him, obey Him, and love Him all the time. It won't be something you try to fake. Love and obedience will come from your heart.

LIVING IT

Sam goes to church and as far as his friends can tell he seems to be a strong Jesus-follower. What they don't know is that when Sam is alone in his own room he doesn't read his Bible. He just doesn't care what it says.

He doesn't pray because he doesn't really think God hears prayers. He doesn't think about salvation because he doesn't believe Jesus is really God's Son or that He came to live, teach, die and come back to life.

April 29

REPENT NOW!

> "Repent, for the kingdom of heaven is near."
> Matthew 4:17

Jesus had a strong purpose for leaving heaven and coming to earth.

Human beings had no chance of knowing God personally because their sin was a wall between God and man.

Jesus came to teach about God's love. He also came to die and to pay the penalty for people's sin – your sin. So, His call is to repent – to turn away from sin – to STOP sinning while there is still time.

You must repent before you die. It's better to admit that you sin sooner rather than later.

LIVING IT

OK, let's be honest. You're a kid and you've got your whole life ahead of you to get serious about living for God. Why not just enjoy life now and do what you want?

There's one very good reason and Jesus said it – the kingdom of heaven is near. No one knows when Jesus will come back to bring people to heaven. Repent now and spend your life loving and serving Him!

April 30

> "How can the guests of the bridegroom fast while he is with them? They cannot, so long as they have him with them."
>
> Mark 2:19

When someone throws a big party, he invites guests to come and celebrate with him. So, would it make sense for the guests to come to the party but refuse to celebrate because they are on diets or something? No way – they can go on diets after the party.

In the same way, why would people refuse to have Jesus be a part of their lives? He is the one throwing the party!

Jesus encouraged people to live lives filled with love for God and others, especially while He was on earth with them.

LIVING IT

Some guys always see a glass as half empty rather than half full. Negative Nickys, huh? Well, some Christians have a doom and gloom approach to life. They look at the badness of the sin in the world or the people who choose to turn away from God and they feel hopeless.

Jesus encouraged His followers to pay attention to His love for them and for everyone and to celebrate all the wonderful things He gives them. Of course, we should pray for those who don't know Him and share His love with them, but don't forget to celebrate Jesus!

May 1

HANGING OUT WITH THE SICK

> "It is not the healthy who need a doctor, but the sick."
>
> Luke 5:31

When Jesus was on earth teaching and preaching, the religious leaders criticized Him for spending time with "sinners." Apparently they didn't believe they were sinners, too.

They thought Jesus should just hang out with them – the religious leaders. He shouldn't rub shoulders with people who didn't believe in God or people who did bad things.

Jesus disagreed because if the religious leaders had faith all figured out, they didn't need Him. But, those who still didn't understand God needed Him.

LIVING IT

Tim understands what Jesus is saying about the sick needing a doctor. He understands that the truth that God loves people is what will help sick people get well. So, Tim finds ways to get to know people who haven't heard yet about God's love. He pays attention to the other guys on his baseball team, to people in his neighborhood and in his class.

Tim wants to pay attention to people who need to know God.

May 2

> "I have come into the world as a light, so that no one who believes in Me should stay in darkness."
>
> John 12:46

You know what it's like to walk into a dark, dark room. You might stub your toe on a chair you can't see or even walk into a wall in the darkness. You just can't see what's going on.

But, even a tiny bit of light reveals what is in the darkness.

Jesus is like that light. He reveals the evil and sin in your heart.

Meeting Jesus is like turning on a light in your heart.

LIVING IT

Before Dan met Jesus his heart was filled with anger.

He was mad at his dad for leaving. Mad at his mom for not making his dad stay. Mad that he wasn't a better baseball player. Mad ... well, just mad.

The thing is that Dan didn't even know he was mad. Until Jesus turned the light on in his heart. Then Dan began to understand what he was dealing with and asked Jesus to help him. The light of Jesus' love turned Dan's life around.

May 3

WHO CARES ABOUT CLOTHES

Jesus knew that people worry about all kinds of things. For example, some guys worry about fitting in with the other guys. They don't want to look too different. Those guys can be pretty mean to the ones who are different in what they like or what they do.

Jesus wants you to know that there are more important things than what you are doing, wearing or even what you're eating and drinking.

Trust Him; that is the most important thing.

> "I tell you, do not worry about your life, what you will eat or drink; or about your body, what you will wear. Is not life more important than food, and the body more important than clothes?"
> Matthew 6:25

LIVING IT

Erik dreads riding the school bus because there are some guys on the bus who pick on him about what he wears, what he does, how he talks, even about how good his grades are. Erik's family doesn't have a lot of money so he doesn't have expensive clothes. But, the cool thing is that Erik trusts Jesus' words. "Life is more than what you wear or what you do or what your grades are. It's more important to be close to Jesus and to be serving Him." It doesn't really matter what those bus guys say!

May 4

"For in the same way you judge others, you will be judged, and with the measure you use, it will be measured to you."
Matthew 7:2

Wow, it's so tempting to be critical of other people, isn't it? It's so easy to judge people who don't like the things we like or that we think they should.

We judge people who don't act like us or the way we think they should.

Jesus' words remind us that judging others is not our business. God is the only one who should judge.

When you are tempted to judge other people, just remember that you will be judged by the same standard you use. Your judge is God, so be careful.

LIVING IT

"Brody gets away with murder," Jude complained to his mom. He felt like Brody was always disobeying their parents and getting away with it! Not that Jude didn't disobey once in a while, too, but he always seemed to get in trouble for it. Anyway, he was glad to point out Brody's failures!

Whew, Jude needs to remember that as he points things out to Mom, the same standards will be used to judge him, too.

May 5

TELL JESUS WHAT YOU NEED

> "What do you want Me to do for you?" He asked.
> Mark 10:36

Two of Jesus' followers came to Him and asked Him if He would do whatever they wanted. Pretty gutsy question, huh?

Jesus didn't just tell them to go away. He asked them what they wanted. Why?

Because Jesus cares about your feelings. He cares about what you want. He cares about your needs. He's willing to listen to what you ask, even if what you ask for isn't good for you.

LIVING IT

Mark has learned to tell Jesus exactly what he needs. His parents have taught him to pray honestly and to believe that Jesus will answer.

So Mark prays for help to obey Jesus. He prays for people who are sick. He asks Jesus to help him do well in school and in sports. He asks Jesus to be a part of every day of his life.

May 6

> "Peace be with you."
> Luke 24:36

Jesus' followers were very sad because He had been murdered. They didn't understand what was going on because they believed He was God's Son. How could He be dead? They were afraid that the same people who killed Him would come after them, too.

Many of them stayed together and tried to stay out of sight. They didn't know what was going to happen without Jesus. But then, suddenly Jesus was there with them; alive, giving them peace.

LIVING IT

It's no fun to be sad. Sadness settles in your heart and takes over your emotions and your attitude. Then everything you do is under the blanket of sadness. Lawrence knows that. His dad moved out and he misses him.

He's kind of scared about what's going to happen to him and his brother and even to his mom. It makes Lawrence feel better when Mom reminds him that Jesus will give him peace if he trusts Him. He knows what's happening and He will take care of all of them.

May 7

SUPER POWER!

"You will receive power when the Holy Spirit comes on you; and you will be My witnesses in Jerusalem, and in all Judea and Samaria, and to the ends of the earth."

Acts 1:8

Jesus' work on earth was finished. He was murdered, but God brought Him back to life. Now, He was going back to heaven. But there was still work to be done on earth.

There were still people who needed to hear about God's love for them. There were still people who needed to be encouraged to repent of their sins and turn to God. So, Jesus told His followers to wait for the Holy Spirit to come.

The Spirit would live in their hearts and help them do Jesus' work all over the earth.

LIVING IT

John loves super heroes. He thinks it would be so cool to have some super power that no one knows about. The thing is, he does! He has the power and strength of God inside of him.

The Holy Spirit is there, strengthening and guiding and with His power John can do anything God wants him to do! How cool is that?

May 8

> "Blessed are the merciful, for they will be shown mercy."
> Matthew 5:7

Much of Jesus' teaching is about how people get along with each other and how people treat each other.

These words were spoken as part of His Sermon on the Mount which is also known as the Beatitudes.

Jesus pointed out that people who show mercy, forgiveness, love and patience to others will be shown mercy by God.

So, treat others the way you want to be treated. Be kind and forgiving and loving.

LIVING IT

Devin picks on Charley all the time. It doesn't matter whether there are other guys around or not. He never really hurts Charley, but he sure makes life miserable for him.

One day at lunch Devin tripped and spilled his lunch tray. Food went everywhere.

Charley could have laughed and made fun of him. But he didn't. He helped Devin pick up the mess and even shared his own food with him. Mercy shown.

May 9

GIVE UP ON ANGER!

> "I tell you that anyone who is angry with his brother will be subject to judgment."
> Matthew 5:22

Why can't people just get along with one another? A lot of Jesus' teaching was about how people treat one another.

Some people make themselves feel better by saying things like, "Well, I've never murdered anyone so I'm not a bad person." But look, Jesus brought His teaching down to the simple statement of "Don't be angry." You will be judged for that.

Try to get along with others. Show love to others – your love and God's love.

LIVING IT

Whoa. This is kind of a scary statement, isn't it? Can you honestly say that you've never been angry with another person?

Yeah, we all have been angry at one time or another. But, Jesus reminds us to make things right with people and settle our differences.

So if you're angry with someone, go to him and work it out. Be at peace with others.

STORING UP TREASURES

> "Do not store up for yourselves treasures on earth, where moth and rust destroy and where thieves break in and steal."
>
> Matthew 6:19

Some people are focused on money. They work to get more and more money. They want more and more stuff – a nicer car, a bigger house, fancier gadgets.

Jesus warns that this is the wrong focus. What you have here on earth is not nearly so important once you realize that it all will be gone one day. Your stuff will get old, break, or even be stolen.

One day you will leave this earth for heaven or hell and none of the stuff you've worked so hard to get can go with you.

LIVING IT

Tommy has learned an important lesson as he has grown up. His parents taught him that money does not buy happiness. Sometimes it's hard because Tommy would like to have some of the cool things that his friends have. But, his parents can't afford those things and that's OK. They are generous with their time and money in serving God and supporting His work and they teach Tommy to do the same thing.

Stuff isn't important, but serving God and helping others is. They are storing up treasures, just not here on earth.

May 11

REAL TREASURES

"Store up for yourselves treasures in heaven, where moth and rust do not destroy, and where thieves do not break in and steal."

Matthew 6:20

What did Jesus mean here? He had just said not to store up treasures on earth, now He says store them in heaven instead. That's weird: How do you deposit money in heaven?

Well, the treasures Jesus was talking about have nothing to do with money. Treasures in heaven are deposited by serving God, loving Him, serving others and helping them, supporting those who do God's work around the world and just generally doing the things that matter to God.

That's heavenly treasure.

LIVING IT

Some people might say that Scott and his family are poor and by the world's standards they are. They don't own their own home, have expensive clothes or fancy electronic gadgets and their car is over 10 years old. But they are missionaries in Africa so their lives are devoted to helping people who are sick and to sharing the message of God's love with them. So the truth is they aren't poor – they are rich in the love of God and people and in the knowledge that they are doing what God wants them to do.

May 12

> "Where your treasure is, there your heart will be also."
> Matthew 6:21

Jesus just came right out and said it – whatever you care about most is what's most important to you.

So, if your goal is to make lots of money or to be famous or powerful then that's what your heart will focus on because that's what you care about most.

You can say you care about things like people who are poor or who don't have clean water to drink, or the HIV/Aids epidemic, but if your day in and day out goal is all about you and what you want and not for the purpose of helping those in need, well, then your heart is not with others but just with you.

LIVING IT

Carl thinks only about himself. He does yard work for neighbors, does extra chores that his parents pay him for but he does these things just to earn money for himself. He wants to buy more things for himself.

Kevin does things to earn money, too. He does a lot of the same jobs Carl does. Kevin has a goal, too. He wants to earn money so he can send it to an organization that is helping get fresh water for people who do not have any. Two guys – two "treasures" – one for self and one for others.

May 13

FORGIVE AND FORGIVE

> "If you forgive men when they sin against you, your heavenly Father will also forgive you."
> Matthew 6:14

There is a bottom line here. If you serve God, your relationships with other people will be affected. What is your response when someone hurts you or cheats you? Do you want to hurt them back or are you willing to forgive them?

Let's say that you won't forgive them, do you still expect God to forgive you when you sin against Him? Yeah that won't work so well for you.

Forgive others if you want to be forgiven ... it's the God way!

LIVING IT

Dave and Ric have been good buddies for a long, long time. But then Ric started hanging out more with Brian. He didn't have time for Dave anymore. Dave was pretty hurt and he didn't understand what happened. After a while though Brian quit hanging out with Ric and Ric was pretty lonely.

Dave could have said, "Serves you right," but he didn't. He remembered what Jesus said about forgiveness so he forgave Ric and they are friends again!

GOD'S CONSTANT CARE

"Look at the birds of the air; they do not sow or reap or store away in barns, and yet your heavenly Father feeds them. Are you not much more valuable than they?"

Matthew 6:26

Think about how God takes care of the birds by making sure they have food. Birds don't have jobs. Birds don't have places to store food but day in and day out God provides what birds and all the other animals need in order to survive.

God loves the creatures He created. More good news: He loves you even more than the animals He made. He will take even better care of you! You can trust Him.

LIVING IT

Now think about this: God loves you very much and He promises to take care of you and supply what you need. Of course, you have to admit that there is a difference between stuff you *want* and stuff you *need* so don't think this means He will give you anything you want. He will give you what you need in order to be taken care of.

Take a minute and thank God right now for providing your needs. Thank Him for His wonderful love.

May-15

TRUE FAITH

> "Do you believe
> that I am able
> to do this?"
> Matthew 9:28

Two blind men called out to Jesus to help them. He stopped and asked them if they really believed that He could restore their sight.

That question is so important. Why would Jesus help someone who didn't really believe in His power?

It's a simple question, but if the men answered honestly (and who would lie to Jesus?) then their lives could be changed forever.

LIVING IT

This is an important question – do you honestly believe that Jesus is able to answer your prayers? Do you believe that He cares enough or is strong enough? Think about the things you ask of him. Are there some big things like healing someone you love who is sick?

Do you pray about big things like helping you find a good friend or for your dad to get a new job? Do you really honestly believe that Jesus can and will answer your prayer? If you don't believe Him, why would He answer?

May 16

GROWING FAITH

"If you have faith as small as a mustard seed, you can say to this mulberry tree, 'Be uprooted and planted in the sea,' and it will obey you."

Luke 17:6

First of all, did you know that a mustard seed is a really, really tiny seed? Jesus is saying that just a tiny bit of faith gives you the power to do amazing things.

What is faith? It is believing and trusting that God is real; that Jesus is God's only Son who died for your sins and was raised back to life by the power of God.

Do you really, truly, honestly believe? The point is that the object (in Jesus' example it is a tree) obeys faith because everything, absolutely everything, is under God's power.

LIVING IT

Jeff would never admit it out loud, but sometimes at night he gets a little scared and wonders if God really does love him and if He really will take care of him. He prays for courage and Jeff learns that faith is something that starts small and grows.

So, he will learn that having a little faith and seeing God answer his prayers leads to more faith so he can trust Him for bigger things. You will learn that, too.

Faith grows and grows as you see God work.

May 17

DOING HARD THINGS

> "My Father, if it is not possible for this cup to be taken away unless I drink it, may Your will be done."
>
> Matthew 26:42

When Jesus prayed these words He knew that He was about to be arrested, tortured and eventually killed; even though He had never done a wrong thing in His life. He would go through all of that simply because of His love for you. It's kind of scary to face things that are hard – even for Jesus.

What's cool about this prayer is that Jesus says, "OK, I'll do it God because it is what You want." He obeyed God and trusted Him to help him get through it.

LIVING IT

Steven's family is moving to a different town that is hundreds of miles from where they live now. Steven is scared. He doesn't want to go, but of course he doesn't have a choice because his dad got a new job and they have to move. Steven knows that his mom and dad pray about every decision they make. They always ask God to help them do what's best for the family. So Steven knows that this move must be God's will. Knowing that, he decides to try to make the best of if and even to be excited about the new friends he will eventually meet.

> "Watch and pray so that you will not fall into temptation. The spirit is willing, but the body is weak."
>
> Matthew 26:41

You will face temptations. There is no doubt about it. Every person will be tempted in some way during his life. Jesus warns you to be careful and use the tools you have available to avoid temptation.

He says to watch – which means pay attention to what you're thinking and doing.

He says to pray – because your strength to resist temptation comes from staying close to God and you do that by prayer. You can try by yourself to resist temptation, but the truth is that you're not strong enough by yourself.

LIVING IT

Alan has started hanging out with guys who have no respect for God. They don't care at all about the Bible or think about how they treat other people. Alan thinks they are a lot of fun because they do things that none of his other friends do. He thinks he can resist the temptation to do the things they do or think the way they think. He thinks he can just hang around them and laugh with them. But, he's wrong. He needs to ask God to help him be strong. He might think about finding new friends, too. He needs to be careful about falling into the temptation to follow their example. Be careful!

May 19

REAL STRENGTH

"I tell you, do not resist an evil person. If someone strikes you on the right cheek, turn to him the other also."
Matthew 5:39

Jesus' message is always the same and it's always based on loving others.

If someone does something mean to you, but you can forgive him and give him another chance, then you are being like Jesus.

So, don't just leap into a fight with someone who does mean things to you. Instead, show Christ's love by not reacting with anger or the urge to get even.

Keep on being kind. Let God take care of all "getting even" things. It's not your problem.

LIVING IT

Jason feels that he looks like a wimp if he doesn't try to get even when someone hurts him. He thinks it looks like he's too chicken to fight back. But actually just the opposite is true.

It takes **more** strength to not react than it does to fight back. So, Jason is showing more strength when he turns the other cheek. He is showing strength that can only come from Jesus, because Jesus says, "Be nice. Take whatever is tossed at you. I'll take care of justice."

May 20

> "Let the little children come to Me, and do not hinder them, for the kingdom of heaven belongs to such as these."
> Matthew 19:14

Isn't this cool? Jesus loves children. One time His disciples wanted to shoo children away so they wouldn't bother Him but Jesus stopped them! He even gave children a big compliment by saying that everyone should have faith like a child.

What does that mean? It means you should have faith that trusts Jesus and believes that what He says is true.

Don't complicate faith in Jesus by challenging everything He says ... trust His actions and His promises.

LIVING IT

It's so cool that Jesus said everyone should have faith like a child. Grown-ups don't usually listen to children or pay much attention to what they say. But because of what Jesus said maybe grown-ups should pay attention to kids.

Is your faith in Jesus childlike? Do you question His teaching? Do you question His love for you or do you just take Him at His word and trust Him ... no matter what?

May 21

THE BLESSING OF FORGIVENESS

"Your sins are forgiven."
Luke 7:48

When a sinful woman came to a home where Jesus was, some people were surprised that Jesus paid any attention to her. But, by the way she treated Him, Jesus knew that she believed He was God's Son and that she had true faith in Him. So Jesus forgave her sins so she could have a friendship with Him and look forward to being in heaven with Him some day.

Forgiving sins is the greatest gift Jesus gives.

LIVING IT

It seems like Brad is always in trouble. No matter how hard he tries to be good he constantly makes bad choices and does the wrong thing. Since people are always reminding him about the wrong things he does and since he is always being punished, Brad has decided that he is a bad boy. He isn't really. He just makes bad choices.

Bible stories like this one show Brad that Jesus loves him and that He forgives the bad things Brad does – his sins. Brad is so happy to know that Jesus forgives him and loves him!

May 22

> "Let's go over to the other side of the lake."
> Luke 8:22

Jesus said this to His disciples just before they got into a boat and started across the lake.

As soon as they sailed, Jesus fell asleep. While He was sleeping a storm blew up and the disciples got scared that the boat would sink. They woke Jesus up so that He could save them. He said, "Where is your faith?"

Why did He say that? Well, think about it – the trip started with His words, "Let's go over to the other side of the lake." He didn't say, "Let's go half way and then sink."

The disciples were Jesus' closest friends but they didn't really trust Him.

LIVING IT

Zach trusts Jesus ... sort of. When life gets hard, his trust gets a little shaky. He is learning, though, that Jesus says what He means and He means what He says. So, just as He meant it when He told His disciples that they were going to the other side of the lake, He means it when He says He loves Zach and will take care of him.

Every time Zach sees Jesus take care of him, the trust in his heart grows a little stronger. Then he is able to trust a little more the next time.

May 23

THE JESUS-WAY

> "Blessed are those who are persecuted because of righteousness, for theirs is the kingdom of heaven."
> Matthew 5:10

People who live the way Jesus teaches sometimes make other people uncomfortable.

When people are uncomfortable they might get a little prickly toward the people who make them feel so awkward. That might lead to a kind of persecution – being picked on just because you want to treat others with kindness, honesty, fairness ... live the way Jesus teaches. So really, you get persecuted for being nice. Weird, huh?

Never fear though, Jesus knows what is happening and He will bless you for choosing to obey Him.

LIVING IT

Jude has a tender heart. He doesn't say bad things about others because he knows it would hurt their feelings if they heard bad things about themselves. However, some of his friends enjoy ripping on other guys for pretty much any reason they can find. Jude doesn't join in their conversation and that made some of them uncomfortable. So now they rip on him! He doesn't care though. He knows that he is behaving in a way that Jesus likes and it makes him feel good that he is being kind to others.

May 24

> "Blessed are you when people insult you, persecute you and falsely say all kinds of evil against you because of Me."
>
> Matthew 5:11

Most people are looking out for Number One ... themselves. They care more about themselves than they do for anyone else. So, when a guy feels his success is threatened by someone he might strike out and try to hurt that person.

Jesus said not to do that. He pointed out that people might try to hurt you just because you love Him. But, you will be blessed by Him if people hurt you because of your faith in Him.

Remember to stay close to Him and He will take care of you.

LIVING IT

Liam was at his friend's house with a bunch of other guys. His friend looked up some websites that Liam knew he shouldn't look at and he said that.

The other guys made fun of him and called him names. Finally Liam just went home. It was hard, but he knew he was doing the right thing by standing up for what he knew was right.

GIVE UP ON WORRY

> "Therefore do not worry about tomorrow, for tomorrow will worry about itself. Each day has enough trouble of its own."
> Matthew 6:34

People worry over things that happened in the past, things that are happening, and things that might happen. Most of the stuff people worry about is stuff that they have no control over and worrying about it will not change a single thing.

What's the solution to worry? God. Yep, keep God's love in the center of your heart. So, when you start worrying about something, you can stop and say, "No. I'm not going to worry about this. I'm going to give it to God and let Him take care of it." Do that every day because every day has its own troubles.

LIVING IT

Aaron is starting at a new school in the fall. He's not very good at making friends and he won't know anyone in the new school. He is worried that he won't be able to make friends. He worries that the guys at this new school might be bullies. He worries about it so much that he is physically ill. Mom gently reminds him that worrying about it won't help. Then they start to pray together every night, asking God to help Aaron make new friends quickly. He feels better because now he knows that God is handling the situation.

May 26

"Not everyone who says to Me, 'Lord, Lord,' will enter the kingdom of heaven, but only He who does the will of My Father who is in heaven."

Matthew 7:21

Have you noticed that some people use God's name, but seem to have no clue who He really is? They may call on Him in a crisis but they aren't really interested in serving Him and they don't love Him. They don't even think about Him much, except maybe when they have a problem.

Jesus says those people shouldn't expect to go to heaven. The people who will go to heaven to live with Him are the ones who obey Him and do what He asks them to do.

LIVING IT

Robert often goes to church with his parents and he used to sit in the back row with his friends. They wrote notes back and forth and whispered. They never heard a single word of the service.

Then, Robert asked Jesus into his heart. He got very serious about learning about Jesus and how to live for Him. Now he sits with his family in church and he listens to every word. Sometimes he even takes notes!

May 27

A FIRM FOUNDATION

You've probably seen news reports about floods that show cars, barns, trees, and houses being swept away in the powerful water.

That is especially true of houses that are not built on firm foundations like rock. The rock won't wash away in the water so the house built on it is safer.

Jesus says that people who hear His teaching and put it into practice in their lives are wise – just like the man who built his house on rock instead of a muddy hillside!

"Therefore everyone who hears these words of Mine and puts them into practice is like a wise man who built his house on the rock. The rain came down, the streams rose, and the winds blew and beat against that house; yet it did not fall, because it had its foundation on the rock."

Matthew 7:24-25

LIVING IT

Do you wonder what these words have to do with you? How do you build a firm foundation? Like this: put the most importance on God and what He thinks and how He wants you to live. Then you are building your life on a firm foundation. If you care more about what friends think and living in a way that makes them happy then your life is built on a weak foundation – like a house built on a muddy hillside that will slide away when strong rains come. Making God and His Word the most important means you are building your life on a strong foundation.

May 28

"Are you so dull?" He asked. "Don't you see that nothing that enters a man from the outside can make him 'unclean'?"

Mark 7:18

What does Jesus mean? He means that nothing you eat or put in your body can make you sin. Sin comes from your heart.

When you decide in your heart to be mean to someone or to cheat while playing a game or taking a test, that is sin. When you choose to tell a lie or do anything else that is disobedient to how Jesus teaches you to live, then your heart is unclean.

LIVING IT

Evan has a bad temper and he knows that he does. He has tried over and over to keep his temper under control but sometimes he just explodes. Evan always tries to blame someone else for his temper outbursts – his brother who makes him mad or a friend who cheats at a game.

Evan can blame others all he wants but the bottom line is that he chooses to let his temper blast. It comes from inside him and the only one who can help him is Jesus.

May 29

LOVING EVERYONE

This is awesome! Jesus challenges His followers to go beyond the friendship line.

Don't just be nice to your friends – be nice to your enemies – people who are not nice to you. Help them any way you can.

Don't worry about getting even. Be even kinder and more helpful to them than you are to your friends. That will show that you are a follower of God because He is kind even to those who do not love Him.

"Love your enemies, do good to them, and lend to them without expecting to get anything back. Then your reward will be great, and you will be sons of the Most High, because He is kind to the ungrateful and wicked."

Luke 6:35

LIVING IT

OK, let's be honest. It's easy and even fun to be nice to your friends. It's fun to do extra nice things for them and to surprise them with special things. But enemies? People who are mean to you or don't like you. Yeah, it's not so much fun to be nice to them, is it?

But, it is what Jesus says to do. After all, anyone can be nice to his friends. But being nice to your enemies – now, that shows you are a Jesus-follower!

May 30

NO-RULES LIVING

> "God did not send His Son into the world to condemn the world, but to save the world through Him."
>
> John 3:17

Some people think that following Jesus means following a long list of rules. That's not true.

Jesus' teachings on how to treat other people, how to treat God, and the right way to live are not just rules that He gave to make life hard. If you follow them, they actually make life more pleasant, relationships better and the world a better place.

LIVING IT

Adam is not good at following rules. In fact He is often in trouble because he doesn't follow rules. So when he thought about asking Jesus into his heart he wondered how he would ever follow all the rules in the Bible.

But, when Adam understood how much Jesus loves him, he decided he could follow the rules. As Adam settled into his relationship with Jesus he realized that the rules were not that big of a deal. Jesus came to make the world a better place and living the way Jesus wants makes Adam happy.

May 31

SOMETHING IN YOUR EYE

"How can you say to your brother, 'Let me take the speck out of your eye,' when all the time there is a plank in your own eye?"

Matthew 7:4

Some people are really critical of others. They pick on people for having the exact same problems they have.

Jesus said, "How can you pick on someone for doing something that you do yourself and possibly even more often that the person you are judging? Take care of your own problems before telling someone else to fix theirs.

LIVING IT

Paul criticizes Norman because he bullies younger guys. That's fine – bullying is not nice. But the thing is that Paul is a bully, too. He picks on younger guys and girls and even bullies kids his own age.

So, Paul shouldn't criticize Norman for doing exactly what he does. Paul doesn't see the problem in himself though, that's why he is critical of Norman. He needs his own eyes opened to his actions.

June 1

FIRST THINGS FIRST

Keep your relationships healthy. Jesus says that God cares about how you and your friends and family get along.

So, if someone is mad at you – whether you did anything wrong or not – work it out. Apologize if you need to. Clear up misunderstandings. Give in if you're being stubborn. Just make sure you and your friend and family are OK.

Once those relationships are good, then give your gifts to God. Don't expect Him to bless you if you aren't doing your part to keep relationships healthy.

"If you are offering your gift at the altar and there remember that your brother has something against you, leave your gift there in front of the altar. First go and be reconciled to your brother, then come and offer your gift."
Matthew 5:23-24

LIVING IT

Sam is really mad at Brent. But, Brent doesn't have a clue as to why, so he just ignores Sam. He goes on with life and does everything he usually does. But as Brent settles down to read his Bible and have a quiet time with God, this verse pops into his mind. He thinks, *maybe I should find out why Sam is so mad at me.* He talks to Sam and discovers it was all a big misunderstanding. Once they talk it through, they are good friends once again. Now, Brent can read his Bible and pray, knowing that his friendship with Sam is healthy again.

June 2

"If you love those who love you, what reward will you get? Are not even the tax collectors doing that? And if you greet only your brothers, what are you doing more than others? Do not even pagans do that?"
Matthew 5:46-47

The best evidence that a guy's heart belongs to Jesus is seen in how he treats other people.

Anyone can be nice to his friends, whether he knows Jesus or not. But, to be nice to people you don't know yet – that's going the extra mile.

It may be scary to talk to someone you don't know but it shows that Jesus is in your heart, filling it with love for all – friends you know and friends you don't know yet.

LIVING IT

Henry is new in town. His family moved in two weeks before school started. In the small town with the small school, everyone knows that he is new and that he doesn't know anyone. Most of the kids just ignore him – look at him kind of weird or look right past him as if he is invisible. Jude is not like the other kids though. He breaks away from his group of friends at lunchtime, introduces himself to Henry and gets to know him. Yeah, it was scary to do that, but Jude thought first about how scared Henry might be to not know anyone.

June 3

HONOR AND RESPECT

"This, then, is how you should pray: 'Our Father in heaven, hallowed be Your name.'"
Matthew 6:9

Jesus knows that some people need things spelled out for them. They need to know exactly what He wants from them.

So, in this verse Jesus begins teaching His followers how to pray. We should not begin our prayer times with requests or complaints or anything other than praise.

Jesus taught us to recognize that God is our Father, our caregiver and we should honor His name. Respect His name above all others. Keep Him in a place of respect and honor as you begin your prayer time.

LIVING IT

Some people pray with a heavy duty case of the "Gimme's." That goes like this: "Dear God, Give me this and do that for me. I want, I want, I want."

Jesus said not to begin prayers like that. He encouraged people to honor God before they begin asking things. Don't look at God as someone who will give you whatever you want. He isn't here just to give you stuff. Honor Him. Respect Him. Trust Him. Recognize that He is God – above all else.

June 4

> "Your kingdom come, Your will be done on earth as it is in heaven."
> Matthew 6:10

This is the second line of what is known as the Lord's Prayer.

Jesus taught that after you recognize God as Father and honor His name, the next step is to be submissive to His will. No wait, not just submissive, but to actually ask that His will be done in your life, in the lives of people you love, in fact all around you.

This recognizes that He is in control of everything on earth, just as He is in heaven.

LIVING IT

Aiden loves God. Well, he says he does but he isn't good at wanting God to have His way in his life. Of course Aiden goes to church. He reads his Bible and of course he prays. But, he doesn't usually say, "Have things Your way, God." No, Aiden tends to tell God what he wants Him to do.

That is not what Jesus taught. He said to give up your own will and just tell God to take over and have things His way. Aiden will learn that eventually.

June 5

ENOUGH FOR TODAY

> "Give us today our daily bread."
> Matthew 6:11

Jesus taught His followers the right way to pray.

It's interesting that His model of prayer did not include a lot of requests for the person doing the praying. His prayer model asks for only what you need for that day.

So Jesus says that you should ask for the food you need for this day; the help you need for this day; the comfort and strength you need for this day – not tomorrow or next week or a year from now.

Trust God to meet your needs one day at a time.

LIVING IT

Alex's parents don't tell him when they are short on money for food and stuff. But Alex can tell when they are worried. He hears them whispering. He notices when Mom says, "Oh I couldn't eat another bite" when she has hardly eaten anything but she pushes more food toward Alex.

He could worry about things, but he doesn't. He just prays the way Jesus taught – "God give us what we need for just today." Alex knows that tomorrow he can (and will) pray exactly that same prayer.

June 6

FORGIVING TO BE FORGIVEN

"Forgive us
our debts, as
we also have
forgiven our
debtors."
Matthew 6:12

These words are also from the Lord's
Prayer we read about earlier. He says we
should ask God to forgive our debts and
our sins. But that is not all.

Jesus said that we must also forgive
those who sin against us. What does that
mean? It means forgive people who hurt you,
cheat you or are mean to you.

How can you expect God to forgive you if you
can't forgive others? If you need help forgiving, ask God
and He will help you.

LIVING IT

Jeremy prays every night before he goes to sleep. Tonight
when he started praying one word kept popping into his mind.
It was a name ... Cal. No matter what Jeremy tried to pray,
Cal's name kept coming into his mind. Finally he understood.

He had been super mad at Cal for a couple of days. Jeremy
knew that God was telling him to let it go and to forgive Cal.
Jeremy knew that was the right thing to do. God forgave him
for lots of stuff every day so he should forgive Cal.

June 7

NO TEMPTATION

> "Lead us not into temptation, but deliver us from the evil one."
>
> Matthew 6:13

The next step in Jesus' example of how to pray is a request for help and protection.

Jesus will not tempt you to do bad things like lose your temper or hurt another person. Those temptations come from Satan. He sneaks into your mind and heart and encourages you to do bad things.

So, Jesus teaches us to pray that God will keep us away from Satan.

LIVING IT

Satan is so sneaky. He knows your weaknesses. Maybe your self-esteem is kind of low, so he sneaks in there and pulls you away from God by making you think negative things about yourself. Satan knows he doesn't have to do big showy things to get you to sin. It's the quiet, little things he does that trip you up.

You may think you can fight him off by yourself, but you can't. He's too strong and too sneaky. So ask God's help. Jesus said that is exactly what you should do!

FUTURE PROMISE

"In My Father's house are many rooms; if it were not so, I would have told you. I am going there to prepare a place for you. And if I go and prepare a place for you, I will come back and take you to be with Me that you also may be where I am."

John 14:2-3

Jesus was trying to get His disciples ready for what was coming – His arrest and murder. He wanted them to realize that none of what was going to happen to Him was pointless.

What He would go through would make it possible for them to be able to join Him in heaven someday.

Jesus promises to come back to earth one day and get His followers so that we can be with Him in heaven. What a wonderful promise!

LIVING IT

Donnie had never thought much about the way Jesus was treated when He was on earth. But then one day his little brother asked him why people were so mean to Jesus. He said that it must have hurt Jesus a lot. Donnie started thinking about Jesus' arrest, torture and death. It helped Donnie to understand the truth of these verses. Jesus and His Father had a plan to make it possible for sinful people (that's everyone) to be able to go to heaven. He promises that we will be with Him. Now Donnie thanks Him every day for this wonderful promise.

THE ONLY WAY TO HEAVEN

"I am the way and the truth and the life. No one comes to the Father except through Me."

John 14:6

There have always been people who teach that there is another way to get to heaven, besides the way Jesus teaches. Those people are wrong.

Jesus made it very clear that the only way to heaven is to believe that He is God's Son, who died for your sins, and now is in heaven with God.

Accepting Jesus as Savior, confessing your sins to Him and inviting Him to live in your heart – that's the only way, the only truth and the only life.

LIVING IT

Mark has asked Jesus to be his Savior. His friend Michael has not. Mark has tried many times to tell Michael about Jesus, but he doesn't want to hear it. Mark has tried to explain that accepting Jesus is the only way to heaven. But, Michael doesn't believe him. "I believe that if I live a good life, if I am kind and honest, then I'll get to heaven. God will let me in for being good," Michael says. He's wrong. Michael is fooling himself and Mark prays that one day Michael will understand that Jesus is the only way to heaven.

> "If anyone loves Me, he will obey My teaching. My Father will love him, and we will come to him and make our home with him."
> John 14:23

Many people mention God's name who may not really know Him.

Athletes thank God for their victories. People who have survived a crisis mention the "Big Guy" who watched out for them. These people might even say they love God. But, Jesus said there is one true evidence that people love Him and that is obedience to Him.

Knowing what Jesus teaches by reading the Bible and then obeying His teachings – that shows real love for Him.

LIVING IT

Scottie wonders if obedience really does show love. "Isn't it possible that I do love Jesus, even if I don't always obey His teachings?" Maybe. After all, everyone disobeys sometimes because no one is perfect. You may disobey without really thinking about it.

The difference is those people who actually love Jesus make the effort to know what Jesus teaches and they try to obey. They even ask Jesus to help them obey. That shows that Jesus really matters to them and that they love Him enough to want to obey.

SEED ON THE PATH

Jesus often told stories to teach His lessons.

One story was about seeds that a farmer sowed. Some of the seed fell on the path and birds ate it before it could take root and grow.

Jesus explained that this example was of people who hear the word of God – the truth – but don't immediately grab it with their hearts and believe it. Then the devil is able to snatch the truth away before they do believe in Jesus.

"A farmer went out to sow his seed. As he was scattering the seed, some fell along the path; it was trampled on, and the birds of the air ate it up. This is the meaning of the parable: The seed is the word of God.

Those along the path are the ones who hear and then the devil comes and takes away the word from their hearts, so that they may not believe and be saved."

Luke 8:5, 11-12

LIVING IT

Timothy has heard about Jesus his whole life. His mom and dad are Christians and have made sure their children hear about Jesus' love for them. But, Timothy hasn't yet taken the time to really think about it or accept Jesus yet. It's OK to take time to think about accepting Jesus and be sure he understands it. But, while Timothy is thinking he has thoughts like *maybe it isn't true* or *why would Jesus love me?* What's happening is that Satan is trying to snatch the truth away from his heart. What should he do? He should talk with his mom and hear the truth again.

June 12

FAITH WITH NO ROOTS

"Some fell on rock, and when it came up, the plants withered because they had no moisture. Those on the rock are the ones who receive the word with joy when they hear it, but they have no root. They believe for a while, but in the time of testing they fall away."

Luke 8:6, 13

This is the second example Jesus gave of seed that a farmer sowed. This seed fell on rock and the plants died because their roots couldn't grow deep and get water.

That's like people who happily accept Jesus as Savior, but they don't grow by reading the Bible and spending time with God.

So, when a crisis comes, they give up. They haven't received the "food" of God's Word to help them grow strong.

LIVING IT

Growing a friendship takes time. The more time you spend with a friend, the better you get to know each other. That's just as true of friendship with Jesus as it is of friendship with people.

As soon as you accept Jesus, get to know Him by reading His Word, praying and just being quiet so you can hear Him speak to you. Then, when life gets tough you know Him well enough to know He will take care of you because you know His promises.

June 13

THE WORRY KING

"Other seed fell among thorns, which grew up with it and choked the plants. The seed that fell among thorns stands for those who hear, but as they go on their way they are choked by life's worries, riches and pleasures, and they do not mature."

Luke 8:7, 14

Thorns and weeds push in front of real plants so they can't get water and food from the soil.

In this example of the seed the farmer sowed, Jesus teaches that people who hear the message of God's love, but still let worry and other things take over their hearts and minds are like those seeds that fell among thorns.

The truth of God's love gets pushed aside by the worries of life so they do not grow strong in their faith.

LIVING IT

Kaleb would never say that he is a worrier. But, he is. He spends time thinking about whether or not he is doing well in school. He is concerned about whether he is a good athlete. He thinks about the health of people he loves.

Why is this stuff considered worry? Because Kaleb spends a lot of time thinking about these things but no time praying about them. He doesn't trust God to help with these things. Kaleb's faith isn't growing because he isn't learning to trust.

June 14

"Still other seed fell on good soil. It came up and yielded a crop, a hundred times more than was sown. The seed on good soil stands for those with a noble and good heart, who hear the word, retain it, and by persevering produce a crop."

Luke 8:8, 15

In the final part of Jesus' story about seeds, He said that some of the seed would fall on good soil. It would take root and get good nutrition that would grow strong, healthy plants.

This part of Jesus' story is an example of people who hear the message of God's love and let it take root in their hearts and grow a strong faith within them. These are healthy Christians who serve God with obedient hearts.

LIVING IT

Oliver did not grow up in a Christian home but when the message of God's love was shared with him, he accepted Jesus right away. His heart was ready to believe and to grow.

Oliver dove into the Bible and read it eagerly, learning as much as he could. He prayed every day and saw answers to his prayers. Oliver's faith grew quickly and soon he trusted Jesus completely!

June 15

HUMBLE HEARTS

> "Blessed are the meek, for they will inherit the earth."
> Matthew 5:5

Another way to read this verse is to replace "meek" with "humble."

So Jesus is saying that a humble person – one who puts others' needs in front of his own will be blessed.

Jesus' teaching is always about love – for others and for God. A guy who is full of pride and concerned only about himself does not show God-based love and concern for others.

LIVING IT

Harry has a generous heart. He doesn't think much about humility. He doesn't have to because it comes naturally to him.

That doesn't mean that Harry doesn't have good self-esteem or confidence in himself. He does. He also has a real concern for other people so he thinks about what others need and how he might be able to help them. He puts others before himself and by doing that shows God's love to them.

LIVING WITH PURPOSE

"The Spirit of the Lord is on Me, because He has anointed Me to preach good news to the poor. He has sent Me to proclaim freedom for the prisoners and recovery of sight for the blind, to release the oppressed, to proclaim the year of the Lord's favor."

Luke 4:18-19

These words of Jesus are very important because He was actually quoting verses from the Old Testament prophet, Isaiah.

Why is that important? Because it shows once again that Jesus cared enough about Scripture to pay attention to it.

Jesus said that He is the person Isaiah was talking about. God sent Jesus to earth with a specific mission.

Accepting Jesus sets you free from many things. He gives freedom.

LIVING IT

Jesus knew why He left heaven and came to earth. He had a purpose. He knew that He had a job to do. Everything Jesus did showed His concern for others. He taught people about God's wonderful love. He did whatever He could to help others – from teaching to healing to raising the dead and forgiving sin.

Serving God and others is what Jesus is all about – what are you all about? What's your purpose today?

THE KINGDOM IS NEAR

> "The kingdom of God is near. Repent and believe the good news!"
>
> Mark 1:15

God's goal is for every person to come to know Him in a personal way.

The only way that can happen is for a person to repent of his sins. That means a person is truly sorry for the bad things he does, even the things he can't stop himself from doing.

He can ask God to help him stop doing those things and make every effort himself to stop.

Believing the good news means believing the news that Jesus died for your sins and was raised back to life by God. He wants to know you and help you.

LIVING IT

Lance has heard the "good news" and his parents are Christians who are very serious about their faith in Jesus. Lance doesn't quite get the "kingdom of God is near"-thing – does that mean his life on earth is going to be short?

Not necessarily. It means that Jesus is returning soon. Therefore, it is important to be a child of God, to be certain in the knowledge that you will be with Him, should tomorrow be the day of His return. Repent and believe and become a part of His kingdom!

"When you pray, do not keep on babbling like pagans, for they think they will be heard because of their many words."

Matthew 6:7

In Jesus' day some people prayed aloud just to show off. They used fancy words and spoke loudly as they kept talking and talking and talking.

They thought it made them look super spiritual if they prayed fancy prayers. But, their prayers were not from the heart. They didn't really care about the things they prayed or about the people around them.

They cared more about what other people thought of them than what God thought. Their fancy prayers did not make God hear their prayers.

LIVING IT

Nicky would never think of praying aloud in public. He is so shy he can barely say hello to someone he doesn't know. The thought of praying aloud in front of other people almost makes him sick. He listens to others pray and notices that they use big words and say things so perfectly. Nicky can't do that. But, his feelings are sincere as he prays for others. Guess what? It doesn't matter whether he can pray with fancy words because God hears what is in his heart. Fancy prayers are fine – if the person praying them truly means them. But, even simple one-word prayers – from the heart – are heard by God.

June 19

RESPECT FOR GOD'S HOUSE

> "Get these out of here! How dare you turn My Father's house into a market!"
> John 2:16

Treat God's house with respect – that's Jesus' message here.

Jesus was in the temple when He said this. There were people in the temple selling animals to be offered as sacrifices. That was normal except they were overcharging and cheating the people so they could make more money.

That made Jesus angry, because the temple should be a place where the people were safe and treated with respect. It was God's house, just as your church is today.

LIVING IT

When the church service was over Brett and some of his buddies went down to the gym for a few minutes. They knew that their parents would be looking for them so they came back up to the sanctuary.

But they forgot that they were in the sanctuary and ran through the aisles, climbed over the chairs and tossed balls of paper to each other. In other words, they showed no respect for God's house.

June 20

> "Give to the one who asks you, and do not turn away from the one who wants to borrow from you."
>
> Matthew 5:42

Jesus said this when He was teaching about the foolishness of trying to get even with other people. Instead of trying to come out on top in every argument or fight, just back off.

You don't always have to win. In fact, when someone, even someone who isn't a friend, wants to borrow something from you or asks you for something, give it to them. In fact, give them more than they ask for.

LIVING IT

Corey is totally weird about his baseball equipment. He doesn't let **anyone** use either of his two mitts or his three special bats. Never. No way. One afternoon his mom came in and asked him to lend one of his mitts to a kid from their church. This guy's family had lost everything they owned in a fire and the boy wanted to play on a team, but they couldn't afford to buy the equipment he needed.

Corey only took a minute to decide – **yes**, he would loan his mitt and one of his special bats, too!

REAL REST

"Come with Me by yourselves to a quiet place and get some rest."

Mark 6:31

Jesus was always surrounded by large crowds of people who wanted to hear Him teach about God or have Him do miracles for them.

It was hard for Jesus and His disciples to have any alone time. Just before Jesus said this, His disciples had told Him that they hadn't even had time to eat. Jesus cared about them just as He cares about you. He knows that sometimes all you need is to get away from the craziness of life and just be alone with Him for awhile. That will give you rest.

LIVING IT

Matt's schedule is crazy. He goes to school; plays in the school band; is on a soccer team; takes tae kwon do lessons; is in youth group ... well, you get the idea. By the end of the day when he has done everything he has to do, including homework, he is so tired he can barely think.

Matt needs rest. He needs to push aside the busyness of his schedule and have some alone time with Jesus. That will give him peace in his soul which will give him the strength to keep on going.

June 22

PROMISES FULFILLED

"Do not think that I have come to abolish the Law or the Prophets; I have not come to abolish them but to fulfill them."
Matthew 5:17

This is so cool. You probably know that the Bible is actually 66 individual books divided into two parts – the Old Testament and the New Testament.

The Old Testament was written before Jesus ever came to earth, but it predicted His coming.

Jesus knew the Old Testament teachings and He announced right here that He was the bridge between the Old and the New. Everything the Old predicted was fulfilled by Jesus! Still today, both parts of the Bible are important.

LIVING IT

Some parts of the Bible are hard to understand, right? So, do you just read the parts you understand? By reading the Old Testament you learn how God takes care of His people. You see how He saves His people so that His word continues through the years.

You will actually understand the whole Bible better as you see how what happened in the New Testament was predicted in the Old. Jesus is the Savior who was promised hundreds of years before He came.

June 23

YOU ARE SPECIAL!

"Suppose one of you has a hundred sheep and loses one of them. Does he not leave the ninety-nine in the open country and go after the lost sheep until he finds it?"
Luke 15:4

Jesus told this story to show how much God loves each and every person. Every single person is important enough to God that He will search high and low to make sure everyone has a chance to know Him.

As Jesus said, God would leave a crowd of people to go look for one follower who has wandered away. He cares about you that much. Awesome, huh?

LIVING IT

Nolan is an average guy of average intelligence and average talents. He doesn't think he is special and no one has ever told him that he is. He looks around and sees kids who are really special. Well, everyone seems to think they are. When he sees these special kids it makes him feel even more invisible. What Nolan doesn't realize is that to God – he is incredibly special – because God loves him. God feels the same way about you! So anytime you feel invisible or not very special, remember that God loves you more than you can possibly imagine!

June 24

TRULY SERVING GOD

> "You will always have the poor among you, but you will not always have Me."
>
> John 12:8

Does this seem like an odd thing for Jesus to say? After all, He's all about caring for others so why would He seem to say to ignore the poor?

Yes, Jesus cares for others and He often taught that people should take care of one another. But He also taught that there is nothing more important than serving God. Loving God. Honoring God.

Do not let anything or anyone become more important than God. If you focus on loving and serving Him then you will do the right things in your life.

LIVING IT

Reed's parents take their children along to volunteer in the food pantry. Reed's special talent is making posters to advertise the need for donations to the pantry. Reed feels like he is doing something good by working there.

He knows that what they do at the pantry helps others with their food needs, but it isn't just helping others that Reed thinks about. He works in the food pantry as a way of serving God.

June 25

THE WORK YOU MUST DO

In the original Greek language, this verse says, "As you are going, make disciples." Jesus wanted His followers to continue the work He had started, of telling people about God's love.

He told His followers to baptize new believers because that identified them as Christians.

The instructions He gave could have seemed overwhelming, but He reminded them that they didn't have to do it alone because He was with them – always.

"Therefore go and make disciples of all nations, baptizing them in the name of the Father and of the Son and of the Holy Spirit, and teaching them to obey everything I have commanded you. And surely I am with you always, to the very end of the age."

Matthew 28:19-20

LIVING IT

These words were not just spoken to instruct the disciples who traveled with Jesus. They were also instructions for Christians of all time. Every single one has the responsibility to share the message of God's love and to teach new believers to get to know Him better so they can obey Him as they live for Him.

It's a big job but you never have to worry that you can't do the work because Jesus is with you ... always.

> "The Son of Man has authority on earth to forgive sins."
>
> Mark 2:10

The religious leaders of Jesus' day constantly criticized Him. They looked for ways to trick Him and even tried to prove that He broke the religious laws of the Old Testament.

Of course, Jesus didn't break any laws because He was without sin. The religious leaders got angry when Jesus forgave people's sins.

He answered their accusations with statements like this proclaiming that He has the authority of God to forgive sins.

LIVING IT

Many times when Jesus forgave someone's sins, He also healed them of some physical problem. He did that because He saw the faith of the people who came to Him.

Faith in Jesus and in the plan for salvation that He gives, brings forgiveness of sin. That makes it possible for you to be with Him in heaven some day. All of this is possible only because Jesus has the authority to forgive sins. What a wonderful gift!

WHO NEEDS A DOCTOR?

The ministry of Jesus focuses on sin.

What is sin? It's the bad, mean or hurtful things that people do. Sin is anything that is disobedient to the way Jesus wants people to live.

But Jesus wants to help sinners to stop sinning. That is what He means when He says He will help the sick. Righteous people do not think they need help. Sinners know they do.

"It is not the healthy who need a doctor, but the sick. But go and learn what this means: 'I desire mercy, not sacrifice.' For I have not come to call the righteous, but sinners."

Matthew 9:12-13

LIVING IT

People who think they never sin are full of pride (which, by the way, is a sin). They think they are so perfect that they do not need Jesus at all. It's very hard for Jesus to help someone like that.

Peter is like that. He says he doesn't ever do anything wrong. So, Peter doesn't pay any attention to Jesus or His teachings. But, Jesus pays attention to Peter because He knows that He is "sick" and needs Him more than anyone!

"If you lend to those from whom you expect repayment, what credit is that to you? Even 'sinners' lend to 'sinners,' expecting to be repaid in full."

Luke 6:34

Once again, Jesus drives home the point that treating others as you would like to be treated is very important.

So what if a guy only treats his friends with respect. Anyone can do that. But if he unselfishly reaches out to those he isn't friends with and shows mercy to them, that is God's love in action.

Mercy helps others and expects nothing in return. It is a different kind of love than that shown by those who do not know Christ.

LIVING IT

Rusty did his own thing. He didn't really care what anyone else thought. So when he started hanging out with Kevin and his friends gave him a hard time about it, he didn't care. "Why do you hang out with Kevin? He's not cool," they said. "No big deal," Rusty said. "He needs help with math and I can help him." "Yeah, but what's in it for you?" they asked.

They simply didn't get it – sometimes helping others in any way you can is just the right thing to do – especially guys who aren't a part of your group. It's Jesus love in action.

June 29

ONLY GOD KNOWS

> "Your Father who sees what is done in secret, will reward you."
> Matthew 6:4

The Christian life is not about showing off. Jesus said that if you do good things just to show off or to get praise from other people, then you've missed the point.

Helping others, being generous, sacrificing for someone else – those are all important things. But, if you live that way just so people will go, "Wow, what a kind and generous person," then that's all the reward you'll get.

Do things privately so that only you and God know about your generosity.

LIVING IT

Mason and his family have a cool tradition. Every so often they make up a box of goodies – non-perishable food items, warm mittens, books, toys for small children – whatever they feel like putting in the box. Then they leave it on the front porch of a family who is struggling financially.

The thing is that no one can know about the gift. It's a secret! It's a nice surprise and helps the family in need. Mason and his family get so much joy from doing it – even though no one knows that they were the givers, except God.

JULY

> "I tell you the truth, no one can enter the kingdom of God unless he is born of water and the Spirit."
> John 3:5

One time a religious leader came to Jesus and asked about the miracles He did.

Most of the religious leaders – the Pharisees – didn't understand the spiritual side of Jesus' teaching because they lived by very strict laws. So, when Jesus said that a person had to be born of the Spirit, it made no sense to them.

When you ask Jesus into your heart the Holy Spirit comes in and lives there, leading, guiding and loving. That makes you a part of God's kingdom.

LIVING IT

This teaching from Jesus is very important because it proves that just doing good things or being a nice person is not enough to get a person into the kingdom of God.

It's wonderful to be nice and do good things, but it isn't enough. The Holy Spirit cleans your heart from sin and makes you a new person on the inside and that's what brings you into God's kingdom.

July 1

THE LIGHT OF THE WORLD

"This is the verdict: Light has come into the world, but men loved darkness instead of light because their deeds were evil."
John 3:19

Jesus is the Light of the world. When His light shines on your heart then you (and others) can see you for what you really are.

Selfishness, hatred, dishonesty, laziness – whatever is in your heart is shown. Some people see themselves for who they really are and ask Jesus to clean up their hearts.

Some say, "Hey, I like the way I am." Those are the ones Jesus is talking about here – the people who like the darkness instead of the light because they like doing evil things.

LIVING IT

Alex thinks that anyone who hasn't stolen anything or hurt anyone is OK. Alex doesn't have some of the bad habits other guys have.

He's OK, but, when his heart is opened to Jesus' words, the light helps him see that he is mean to his little brother for no reason and that he sometimes lies to his mom. Yeah, there is stuff in Alex's heart that he needs Jesus to clean up.

July 2

LIGHT CHANGES THINGS

"Whoever lives by the truth comes into the light, so that it may be seen plainly that what he has done has been done through God."

John 3:21

If a person lives by the truth, then he has nothing to hide. So he is willing to step into the light even though everything about his life will be revealed – the good and the bad.

He is willing to let everybody see that who he is and the changes in his heart and life are all due to Christ and His power and love.

His good deeds are because of Jesus and the improvements in his thoughts and actions are because of Him.

LIVING IT

When Zach asked Jesus to be his Savior, Jesus showed him some things in his heart that needed to be changed. One of those was the way Zach treated his parents. He was rebellious toward them and argued with them about pretty much everything.

His parents did not know Jesus and Zach has a chance to be a witness to them. So he went to them and said, "Mom, Dad, I asked Jesus into my heart and He showed me that I've not treated you very well. I just want you to know that I'm sorry and with His help, I will do better."

FIRST PLACE IS GOD'S

> "Love the Lord your God with all your heart and with all your soul and with all your mind. This is the first and greatest commandment."
>
> Matthew 22:37-38

Jesus left no room for compromise with this command. He made it as clear as He could.

Love God completely. Love God totally. Give Him your heart – your emotions. Give Him your soul – your being. Give Him your mind – your thoughts.

God will not share first place in your heart, soul and mind with anything else. He is to be Number One. You will never be sorry.

LIVING IT

James has heard this verse about a bazillion times. He understands that God must have first place above all other things in his heart, soul and mind. He thinks he has accomplished that. But, James doesn't see that something in his heart keeps knocking God out of first place – his friends.

Yeah, James cares very much about what his friends think about him. Sometimes they are even more important than God. Yikes. Time to fix that, right? First place in his heart, soul and mind must belong to God alone!

July 4

> "The second [commandment] is like it: 'Love your neighbor as yourself.' All the Law and the Prophets hang on these two commandments."
>
> Matthew 22:39-40

Love. Love. Love. Jesus had just taught His followers that loving God with all their heart, soul and mind was the greatest commandment.

Now, He says that the second greatest commandment is to love others. Basic stuff. These two commands are basic to everything else He teaches.

This totally blasted the Pharisees' teachings that living for God meant obeying lots of rules, especially if those rules showed no love to God or others. Love is what it's all about.

LIVING IT

It's tempting to judge other people for what they say or do. Ross knows that first hand. He totally dropped one friend because of the way the guy acted. Ross knows that this friend has a messy family situation and he doesn't know Jesus.

What Ross learns from this command of Jesus is that he should love his friend. Love, love, love. Love in a way that doesn't expect anything in return. Look beyond the unkind words or actions and see what might be causing them. Just love.

July 5

SOURCE OF PEACE

> "Peace I leave with you; My peace I give you. I do not give to you as the world gives. Do not let your hearts be troubled and do not be afraid."
>
> John 14:27

Life is stressful. At times the problems are overwhelming.

There are people who attack you for who you are, what you believe and how you live. Sometimes people attack you simply because you are a Jesus-follower.

Never fear, Jesus knows that and encourages you to stick close to Him. He gives real peace, not the kind of peace that comes from agreeing with other people, but real peace that settles deep in your soul.

LIVING IT

David has never really experienced peace. There isn't anything like that in his family. He looks at some of his friends' families and it seems like they hardly ever have problems. But his problems seem to go from one crisis to another. It's hard for David to know peace when his parents are stressed about money or a sick parent or rebellious kids.

Where does David find peace? Jesus. He can tell Jesus anything that is worrying him. Jesus cares. And if David can trust Him, Jesus will give David peace in his heart.

> "My prayer is not that You take them out of the world but that You protect them from the evil one."
>
> John 17:15

Jesus knows that Satan is going to attack people who try to obey Him. He will do everything in his power to stop their obedience. He will even make them question God's love for them. He will try to make them think that they're not good enough for God to love.

Jesus knew that would happen so why didn't He ask God to take Christians out of the world? Because, Christians have work to do here – telling others about God's love.

So, Jesus didn't ask God to take Christians to heaven, but He did ask God to protect them from Satan.

LIVING IT

Landon has claimed this prayer and asked God to do it in his life. He knows God is answering, too. How does he know? He knows that when negative thoughts about himself pop into his mind – about how he isn't any good at things – just as quickly an encouraging thought comes along. He knows that it has to be God protecting him.

Landon is so thankful for God's protection and so thankful that He is more powerful than Satan!

July 7

JESUS' BROKEN HEART

> "My soul is overwhelmed with sorrow to the point of death. Stay here and keep watch with Me."
> Matthew 26:38

Jesus took His disciples with Him to the Garden of Gethsemane on the night He was arrested. He knew what was going to happen – betrayal, arrest, torture, death.

Why was His soul overwhelmed with such sorrow? Because of the pain that was ahead for Him? Maybe. But He probably felt sadness, too, that the people who heard Him teach and knew of His miracles still rejected Him and the message of God's love.

That broke His heart.

LIVING IT

One of Max's favorite songs has a line in it that says, "Break my heart with what breaks yours" and he often prays that thought. Max doesn't want to be a surface Christian. He wants his faith to go deep in his heart and he wants to love others the way Jesus wanted.

So, he asks God to make his heart sensitive to the things that break God's heart and then to show him how to be a help to God's work.

July 8

> "Everyone who asks receives; he who seeks finds; and to him who knocks the door will be opened."
>
> Matthew 7:8

Jesus wants you to take prayer seriously because prayer seriously makes a difference. That's why He made the point of telling you that asking, seeking and knocking brings results.

Keep your heart focused on God so that the things you ask, seek and knock for are in line with His will and not selfish or self-centered.

LIVING IT

July 9

Tate has a serious case of the "I wants." His prayers are long lists of "I want this" or "Do that for me." He doesn't feel guilty because Jesus said to ask for whatever he wants. Yeah, well Tate doesn't really understand Jesus' instructions. His prayers are mostly focused on himself.

Tate needs to see the whole picture of desiring God's will to be done and wanting to serve Him with his whole heart. Jesus often says to be focused on loving God and others. Love, that's what should guide his prayers.

BRIGHT LIGHTS

"Neither do people light a lamp and put it under a bowl. Instead they put it on its stand, and it gives light to everyone in the house."

Matthew 5:15

Jesus is the Light of the World and in the verse just before this one He says that those who believe in Him are also lights in the world.

Jesus knows that life as a Christian is not easy. You may not always be treated kindly by those who do not share your beliefs.

However, He doesn't let Christians off the hook – He doesn't say, "Well don't worry about things. Just keep quiet about your faith." Nope, He says to let your light keep shining – do not hide it. Your light is **His** light and it will light the way for many people!

LIVING IT

Vince is a brand-new Christian and he is super excited about his new relationship with Jesus. He is so excited that he wants to tell all his friends about Jesus. But, some of Vince's friends don't want to hear about his faith and they get pretty snarky toward him. They say some pretty mean things to him.

Vince could just be quiet and go on with his life – but he doesn't. He keeps sharing his faith, but is careful to do it kindly and with respect. Vince knows that he is Jesus' light to his friends!

July 10

"I tell you the truth, until heaven and earth disappear, not the smallest letter, not the least stroke of a pen, will by any means disappear from the Law until everything is accomplished."

Matthew 5:18

Jesus respects the Scriptures. Because He understands Scripture from God's viewpoint, He always told people, while He was on earth, how important Scripture is.

Here He emphasizes the complete truth of Scripture and that not one word of it will change until everything it says actually happens. Pretty good reason to study Scripture, huh?

LIVING IT

Jim has asked Jesus to be his Savior. His parents celebrated by giving him a new Bible. But, Jim tossed the Bible on his desk and it has stayed there ever since. Now it's covered under a pile of papers and magazines. He has never opened it.

Jim is a Christian, but he isn't growing or learning because he is ignoring God's Word. Jim does not understand how very important God's Word is. He just doesn't get it.

July 11

OBEYING NO MATTER WHAT

Jesus was very clear about the necessity of honoring Scripture. God doesn't take disobedience lightly. He urges, encourages and expects His children to know and obey Scripture.

It makes life better. It leads to better relationships with others, honor toward God, self-respect and care for yourself. It makes sense.

Those who honor Scripture will be honored in heaven. Those who do not and encourage others to also disobey will answer for that in heaven.

"Anyone who breaks one of the least of these commandments and teaches others to do the same will be called least in the kingdom of heaven, but whoever practices and teaches these commands will be called great in the kingdom of heaven."

Matthew 5:19

LIVING IT

Dario had known for a week that a super big math test was going to happen on Friday. But he hadn't bothered to study for even a half hour. When he got to class Dario leaned over to his buddy Jaden and said, "Do me a favor and slide your test paper over a bit so I can see your answers. OK?"

Jaden wasn't even tempted. He knew that would be cheating and he didn't want to encourage Dario's dishonesty. Jaden is honoring Jesus' words by not encouraging someone else to sin.

July 12

MAKING PEACE

"Settle matters quickly with your adversary who is taking you to court. Do it while you are still with him on the way, or he may hand you over to the judge and the judge may hand you over to the officer, and you may be thrown into prison. I tell you the truth, you will not get out until you have paid the last penny."

Matthew 5:25-26

Jesus encourages healthy relationships with the people around you. So, if someone says that you have hurt him or cheated him – go to him and settle the problem. You take the lead and talk with him to set things right.

What happens when you ignore problems? They will grow into bigger and bigger problems, which will take a lot more time and energy to solve and probably involve a lot more people.

LIVING IT

Ben and Garrett got into an argument over something that really wasn't a big deal. But they didn't settle their problem and it grew into a giant fight. Their friends had to choose sides because they couldn't be friends with both guys.

Both boys are Christians and they know what Jesus says about settling problems. Finally Ben and Garrett sat down and talked through their problem. They settled their differences and let all their friends know so that everyone could be friends again.

July 13

TOTAL FORGIVENESS

This is hard, isn't it? Forgiving someone who has hurt you is not an easy thing to do. It's a lot easier to try to get even with the one who has hurt you or even to ignore him. You might even pat yourself on the back for ignoring him, like that is the Christian thing to do.

Actually, the Christian thing is to forgive the person who hurts you. Totally, completely forgive him. After all, God forgives you when you hurt others or Him. He forgives you over and over and over.

LIVING IT

Brandon won the spelling bee at school. Allen has won it for the last few years and this year he is not a good loser. He has loudly accused Brandon of cheating (which isn't true) to all their friends. Brandon is angry at Allen for calling him a cheater.

But, he remembers Jesus' teaching and chooses to obey. He forgives Allen and doesn't try to get even. After a while Allen calms down and then apologizes to Brandon. Brandon did the right thing – the Christian thing.

July 14

WHOSE PRAISE DO YOU WANT?

"When you fast, do not look somber as the hypocrites do, for they disfigure their faces to show men they are fasting. I tell you the truth, they have received their reward in full."

Matthew 6:16

Don't do things for show. When you fast or pray or serve or do anything that is supposed to be for God, don't try to make it all about you by drawing attention to yourself.

Don't try to look like you are starving when you are fasting. Don't try to get people to feel sorry for you or try to make people think you are awesomely spiritual. If you do that, don't expect God's blessings.

The only reward you are going to get is whatever people say about you.

LIVING IT

Some guys always want to be the center of attention. They want to be the funniest, the smartest or the strongest. These guys want everyone to notice if they are hurt or sick. They want cheers for when they sing well or do well in sports or anything else. The bottom line is they want a pat on the back for anything they do. Even when they are doing something good for other people, they want everyone to see it and cheer for them.

Guys like this miss the main point of serving God. They are looking for praise from people, not from God.

July 15

BETWEEN YOU AND GOD

Jesus says some things should just be between you and God – no one else should watch or even know about them.

Fasting is a time when you choose not to eat, and instead spend time in prayer and focusing on God. It's no one else's business that you are fasting.

If you are concerned about what others think of you, then you aren't really focused on God, are you?

"When you fast, put oil on your head and wash your face, so that it will not be obvious to men that you are fasting, but only to your Father, who is unseen; and your Father, who sees what is done in secret, will reward you."

Matthew 6:17-18

LIVING IT

What does it really mean to be focused on God? Well, you know what it's like to be focused on something you enjoy, whether it's music, sports, reading, hanging out with friends or practicing hobbies, right? You think about that thing all the time and you want to be doing it constantly.

Being focused on God is like that because you think about Him, read His Word, pray, and try to understand what He wants for you. This is not stuff for other people to be involved in. It is just between you and God.

> "Who of you by worrying can add a single hour to his life?"
> Matthew 6:27

Worry can suck energy right out of your life. It takes away hope. It smothers joy. Here's what's scary though – worry means you don't trust God.

Trust and worry can't live in the same heart. If you honestly believe that Jesus loves you and that His Word is true, then what do you have to worry about?

LIVING IT

Not worry? Seriously? How can I not worry? Mark thought. *I know that Jesus said not to worry but He didn't know what was going to happen to my family, did He? He probably expects me to worry.*

No, Mark, He doesn't. It may be hard to believe but Jesus is not surprised by anything that happens to you. He can take care of you and handle any problem that comes up. So, save your energy. Don't worry. Just let Jesus take care of things.

July 17

WHAT DO YOU NEED?

The thing about worry is that most of the things people worry about are things they have no control over.

God knows what your needs are even before you know what they are. Just before this Jesus pointed out how God takes care of the flowers in the field. He makes them grow, watches over them and they are beautiful. He loves you even more than

He loves those flowers, so trust Him!

"So do not worry, saying, 'What shall we eat?' or 'What shall we drink?' or 'What shall we wear?' For the pagans run after all these things, and your heavenly Father knows that you need them."
Matthew 6:31-32

LIVING IT

Todd doesn't worry about clothes. As long as he has something to wear, he doesn't care if it's dirty, old or ragged. He just wants to get outside and play with his friends.

Does that mean that Todd doesn't worry? Yeah, but he worries about other things. Todd worries about whether his friends are going to dump him or whether he will make the baseball team or what will happen if his dad loses his job. There will always be something to worry about unless Todd chooses to trust Jesus to take care of everything. Yeah, that's the best thing.

July 18

"Seek first His kingdom and His righteousness, and all these things will be given to you as well."
Matthew 6:33

Keep your eyes on what is really important. Some people worry about everyday things like food or clothes. Some worry about money and success. Some worry about what other people think of them.

Jesus said not to worry about any of that stuff. He said to keep your eyes on the goal of knowing and serving God and not to worry about any of the other stuff.

Jesus will take care of everything you need.

LIVING IT

Some of Jack's friends spend all their energy working at "stuff." Some want to be the best basketball player ever so they practice all the time. Some want to be great musicians so they practice a lot. Some plan to be successful businessmen ....

Jack has learned to keep his focus on God. He studies the Bible to know God better. He prays and seeks God's guidance in his life. He knows if he is obeying and serving God that everything else will fall into place.

July 19

EYE TROUBLE

"You hypocrite, first take the plank out of your own eye, and then you will see clearly to remove the speck from your brother's eye."

Matthew 7:5

Jesus' teachings are mostly about relationships with others and fairness and treating others well.

So this command is to not criticize your friends or family members for the small things they do that bug you.

Instead, look at the things you do that hurt others. You will probably find that your actions are worse than the actions of others. Take care of yourself and don't worry about others.

LIVING IT

"Billy is such a loser," Kenny tells everyone. "He wants everyone to pay attention to him. When he is around no one pays attention to anyone else. It makes me crazy. He can't stand it if anyone else is the center of attention!" Kenny may be right about Billy, but what he isn't admitting to himself is that he is jealous of Billy because he wants more attention himself!

Yeah, Kenny, take care of your own weaknesses before you criticize someone else.

July 20

PROTECT THE IMPORTANT

"Do not give dogs what is sacred; do not throw your pearls to pigs. If you do, they may trample them under their feet, and then turn and tear you to pieces."

Matthew 7:6

What is the most valuable thing you have to give to another person? Guess what, it's not any of your stuff. It is your heart and loyalty. Jesus said to be careful where you place your heart and loyalty. If you give it to someone who doesn't deserve it, he might not respect your loyalty. He might trample it and totally wreck it. He will not have any concern for you or what's best for you. Give sacred things (like your heart) only to the One who deserves it – God.

LIVING IT

Dan is sort of the leader of his group of guys. They all do what he says even though they don't really like him. They are more scared of him. The guys who are afraid of him give all their loyalty to Dan, because they are afraid they won't have any friends if they don't. But, Dan doesn't care about his "friends" at all. He only cares about himself. So, he takes the guys' loyalty and devotion and pretty much just throws it away. He doesn't care about their problems or what is good for them at all.

July 21

GOD'S WONDERFUL GIFTS

"Which of you, if his son asks for bread, will give him a stone? Or if he asks for a fish, will give him a snake? If you, then, though you are evil, know how to give good gifts to your children, how much more will your Father in heaven give good gifts to those who ask Him?"

Matthew 7:9-11

God loves you more than you can possibly imagine. Jesus really wants you to understand that and believe it.

As much as your parents love you and give you wonderful gifts, God loves you more and wants to give you everything you need and even things you don't need – blessings beyond anything you can ask or dream.

LIVING IT

Calvin reads this verse and thinks, *Yeah, right.* After all, he doesn't have **everything** he wants, not even close. He looks around at his friends and sees that he doesn't have all the stuff they have. Calvin doesn't get the meaning of what God's good gifts are. That's because God's gifts aren't "stuff." They are love, joy, hope, peace, help, protection, and the promise of heaven. Sometimes His gifts are beautiful flowers, rainbows or the smile from a loved one that remind you that God is with you, loving you more than you know.

July 22

DO UNTO OTHERS

> "So in everything, do to others what you would have them do to you, for this sums up the Law and the Prophets."
> Matthew 7:12

Jesus teaches His followers to treat other people well. He knows that it's easy to get caught up in selfish attitudes and think only about how things affect you. When that happens you start treating other people badly. Don't do that.

Treat others the way you want them to treat you – then even if they aren't nice back, your conscience is clear. And they just might begin to treat you as nicely as you treat them!

LIVING IT

Joey and Tony are both soccer players. They are both good goalies, but Joey is just a bit better and wins the starting position as goalie. Tony is jealous and starts making nasty comments to Joey and treating him in a rotten way. He even spreads some false rumors about Joey – yeah, it gets ugly.

Joey's response could be to treat Tony mean right back. But it isn't. Instead he is consistently kind to Tony. He treats Tony the way he would like to be treated. After a while, Tony gets over his anger and jealousy and apologizes to Joey. They are friends again. That's the Jesus-way.

July 23

THE PATH TO LIFE

> "Small is the gate and narrow the road that leads to life, and only a few find it."
>
> Matthew 7:14

Jesus knows that the road to life with Him – the road to heaven – will not always be the popular way with all people.

Those who aren't interested in knowing Jesus walk together down a wide road that may seem like the easy way. But, it doesn't lead to life with Jesus. It's comfortable because you are traveling with a crowd, but it's a crowd going nowhere.

Pay attention to Jesus and to God's Word and find the narrow road that leads to life with Him.

LIVING IT

Why is the road to heaven called the narrow way? Brian wondered about it so he asked his dad. His dad explained that the wide road seems to have fewer rules and there is a whole gang of people on it. The narrow road is narrow because fewer people choose it and it means obeying Jesus' teachings. It may appear to have more rules, but it really teaches the best way to get along with others and to serve God. Brian chooses the narrow road – to some it appears to be the harder way to go – but in the end it leads to life with Jesus.

July 24

"Every good tree bears good fruit, but a bad tree bears bad fruit. A good tree cannot bear bad fruit, and a bad tree cannot bear good fruit."
Matthew 7:17-18

Jesus often uses the illustration of trees and fruit. He makes it an example of a Jesus-follower's life.

Basic – a healthy tree has healthy, good fruit but an unhealthy tree has unhealthy, bad fruit.

A person who has Jesus in his heart should have good fruit which is love and respect for God and love and compassion for others. A person who doesn't have Jesus in his heart will not have good fruit.

LIVING IT

It's true that people who do not know Jesus can be kind and loving sometimes. But, there is a depth to a Christian's love that makes him unselfish and generous even to people he doesn't know or people who might be considered "enemies." It's "good fruit" that comes from Jesus' love.

Andy's life shows good fruit – he encourages others to succeed and be in the spotlight instead of himself. He gives time and energy to teach younger kids how to play sports. He plays with his neighbor's kids so the mom can do chores. Good fruit that comes from Jesus.

July 25

TRUTH FRUIT

> "By their fruit you will recognize them."
>
> Matthew 7:20

There were people in Jesus' day (as there are today) who talk a good talk about knowing God. They announce how they trust "the big guy upstairs" or call for prayer during a crisis. But, these people may not know God at all.

How do you know? Look at the "fruit" of their lives. If they treat others with respect and love, and have a consistent relationship with God, that shows good fruit. If they put others before themselves and truly care about others, then they may know Jesus.

If they only acknowledge Him in a crisis or a big victory – then maybe not.

LIVING IT

Michael is a good long-distance runner and every time he wins a race he shoves his arm in the air and thanks the "big guy" for helping him win. Is Michael a true Christian? Well, that is only for God to judge, but the evidence in his life of whether he shows care and compassion for others and kindness and helpfulness to them tells the truth.

Also, his devotion to God by reading His Word and praying shows that God is a daily presence in his life. Always know that the fruit in your life shows the truth in your heart.

July 26

THE REAL THING

"Many will say to Me on that day, 'Lord, Lord, did we not prophesy in Your name, and in Your name drive out demons and perform many miracles?' Then I will tell them plainly, 'I never knew you. Away from Me, you evildoers!'"

Matthew 7:22-23

Choosing to follow Jesus is a serious decision. Choosing not to follow Jesus is even more serious.

Jesus makes it very clear that fakers don't fool Him. People who claim to do God's work but have not accepted Jesus as Savior are fakers. They may do wonderful acts of kindness and fool others, but when it comes to entering heaven they will find they haven't fooled Him. If they don't know Jesus, they don't enter heaven.

LIVING IT

Devin goes to church. He knows Bible verses, goes on mission trips and is part of a ministry team at his church. He does Christian things and by outward appearance is a wonderful Christian.

But Devin hasn't asked Jesus into his heart. He hasn't confessed his sins to Him. Devin likes doing Christian stuff because it makes him feel good. But he doesn't know the Savior. So, on the day when he wants to enter heaven, he will be turned away. It's not too late for Devin though – he can still ask Jesus to be his Savior!

July 27

FIRM FOUNDATION

Following Jesus' teachings gives peace and purpose to life because you know that you can trust Him. It's a firm foundation. In the tough times of life those who don't trust Jesus find that they have no foundation. If you've ever stood on a beach you know what it feels like when the water comes up over your feet and pulls the sand away. Like a house built on sand, when a storm comes the rain pulls the sand away and the house crashes down. If your foundation is not firm (on God) then it will be pulled away in the storms of life.

"Everyone who hears these words of Mine and does not put them into practice is like a foolish man who built his house on sand. The rain came down, the streams rose, and the winds blew and beat against that house, and it fell with a great crash."

Matthew 7:26-27

LIVING IT

Teddy found out what the term "firm foundation" means. His dad lost his job and after a while they had to move out of their house. They moved in with his grandparents and his parents were so sad and quiet.

Teddy was scared. He was worried about his parents because they were fighting a lot. He missed his friends in their old neighborhood. But, Teddy trusted God. He believed God would take care of them so his firm foundation on Jesus' love carried him through the hard times.

July 28

JOB OPENINGS!

"The harvest is plentiful but the workers are few. Ask the Lord of the harvest, therefore, to send out workers into His harvest field."
Matthew 9:37-38

Jesus stayed focused on the reason He left heaven to come to earth and that was so people could know God personally.

When He said this, He knew there were many people who didn't yet know God; many people who had not accepted Jesus as Savior.

Jesus wanted every person to have an opportunity to hear about God's love – every person for all time. He needs workers – you for example – to make this happen.

Jesus calls for workers and for His people to ask God to send more and more workers.

LIVING IT

When Caden reads this verse it challenges him. He has friends and family members who do not know Jesus. Of course Caden prays for them to come to know Him, but is there more he could do?

Yes, Caden looks for chances to share his faith in Jesus and tell his friends and family members how much Jesus means to him. Caden prays for people in other countries who have never had a chance to hear about God's love and he thanks God for the missionaries who dedicate their lives to go to those places and share God's love.

July 29

LIFE TO THE FULL

> "Whoever finds his life will lose it, and whoever loses his life for My sake will find it."
>
> Matthew 10:39

This is kind of a confusing statement, isn't it? Focus on the words "whoever loses his life will find it."

Losing your life – giving it over to Jesus doesn't actually take your life away. No, it makes your life matter by giving it purpose and peace and joy. So, actually your life is found and it's better than before.

LIVING IT

Phil always had a dream to be a professional musician. He writes music and is a good singer. He doesn't have to throw that dream away. After all, God gave him that talent.

But the way he "finds his life for Jesus' sake" is that he dedicates his music talent to Jesus. Now the songs he writes are about living for Jesus and serving him. Phil still sings, but his focus is Jesus.

July 30

HUMBLE CHILDREN

"I praise You, Father, Lord of heaven and earth, because You have hidden these things from the wise and learned, and revealed them to little children. Yes, Father, for this was Your good pleasure."
Matthew 11:25-26

The religious leaders of Jesus' day thought they knew everything. They thought they had all the answers about God and that they were living for Him.

But, Jesus knew they didn't. He knew that the simple faith of a child was more pleasing to God than the arrogant religious leaders.

God lets those who have faith like little children understand more than those who think they have all the answers.

LIVING IT

Joey doesn't understand a lot about the Bible or living for God so he never says much about his faith. He knows some older guys who think they have it all figured out. They're always saying things like, "God told me this" or "The Bible says." The truth is they don't have anything figured out. They are kind of making up their own version of Christianity.

Humble guys like Joey understand a lot more than the showy guys. God opens their minds and hearts so they can understand.

"If any of you has a sheep and it falls into a pit on the Sabbath, will you not take hold of it and lift it out? How much more valuable is a man than a sheep! Therefore it is lawful to do good on the Sabbath."

Matthew 12:11-12

Mercy is at the heart of Jesus' message. Some people said that the only right way to follow God was to live by a bunch of rules.

Jesus didn't agree with that. He taught that it shows more of God's love to take care of people when they need something – even when that help seems to break a law of God.

Caring for others shows God's love.

LIVING IT

The Pharisees of Jesus' time loved to live by rules. They had a long list of rules and they insisted everyone had to obey their rules. Some of the rules were in the Bible. Some were not.

But, what the Pharisees missed was that some rules – like no work on the Sabbath – just didn't make sense if someone was in danger and needed help. Aren't you glad that Jesus feels people are more important than rules?

August 1

CARELESS WORDS

> "I tell you that men will have to give account on the day of judgment for every careless word they have spoken."
>
> Matthew 12:36

The words you say reflect what is in your heart. Jesus is very clear about this. That's why He notices every word you speak and it is why you will have to give a reason for everything you say.

That includes things you say because you think they're funny or because you're angry or because you're tired. Every word.

LIVING IT

Drew loves to make other guys laugh. He likes that he is known as the funny one in his crowd. That's OK, except sometimes his funny words are at the expense of someone else. He makes friends laugh by commenting on another guy's lack of muscles or how smart he is. Sometimes he even makes off-color remarks because it makes the guys laugh. After reading these words of Jesus Drew knows that the words he thought didn't hurt anyone – do hurt someone – him! He will have to take responsibility for them.

August 2

> "Blessed are your eyes because they see, and your ears because they hear."
>
> Matthew 13:16

Jesus had just finished talking about people who think they have all the answers.

People like that are so full of pride in themselves that they can't hear what anyone else says. They can't see how arrogant they are. They are so blinded that they can't even see the love of God around them.

They are blind and deaf to everything except themselves and their rules.

LIVING IT

Marcus is a new Christian. He just accepted Christ a few weeks ago and is excited about everything he is learning about living for God. Marcus had always thought that the Christian life was only about following a long list of rules. He had been afraid that it meant not having any fun at all.

But, as he reads his Bible and talks with older Christians, Marcus's eyes are opened to the unbelievable love of Christ. That's what he sees in His teachings, His miracles, in every way He lived His life! That's what Marcus wants to show in his life, too. Love for God and love for others.

THE GROWING KINGDOM

> "The kingdom of heaven is like yeast that a woman took and mixed into a large amount of flour until it worked all through the dough."
>
> Matthew 13:33

Sometimes it seems as though the bad guys are winning. Bad news of terrible crimes fill the news. Evil people seem to get more powerful and richer.

But in the middle of all that bad stuff is God's kingdom – quietly working its way into the hearts of people and spreading all through the world.

Don't worry about the bad guys winning, because just like yeast that silently makes bread rise, God's kingdom will win over evil one day.

LIVING IT

Sometimes the TV news reports make Evan nervous. He wonders why people are so mean to each other. Bad things happen right in the town where he lives. People steal from others. Kids get hurt and people are killed. The news from around the world is even worse. But Evan's mom reminds him that God is still working, even through all the scary stuff. Every day more people accept Jesus and their hearts are changed to kindness and love. Evan and Mom pray every day for God's kingdom to keep growing so more and more people know Him.

August 4

"'No,' he answered, 'because while you are pulling the weeds, you may root up the wheat with them. Let both grow together until the harvest. At that time I will tell the harvesters: First collect the weeds and tie them in bundles to be burned, then gather the wheat and bring it into my barn.'"

Matthew 13:29-30

Jesus knows that some people will choose to accept Him as Savior and follow Him. Those people are the "wheat" in this parable. People who deny that He is Savior and choose not to follow Him are the "weeds."

People who do not follow Christ follow Satan. Both groups live together on earth, but when the Day of Judgment comes the "weed" people will not enter heaven. By their own choice they have denied Jesus and will not spend eternity with Him.

LIVING IT

This statement from Jesus really touches Steve's heart. He has accepted Jesus and is certain that he will someday be in heaven with Him.

But, Steve's mom, dad and brother do not know Jesus. The idea that they will not be with him in eternity makes him sad. Steve prays for his family every day. He looks for opportunities to share his faith with them and to show them Jesus' love by the way he treats them.

August 5

CARING FOR BASIC NEEDS

Some people would have you believe that Jesus only cares about your soul – spiritual things.

But, these words show that it isn't true. He cares about your whole life – even something so basic as whether or not you are hungry.

How can you concentrate on listening to Jesus or growing in your faith if you are really, truly hungry? Jesus wants those basic needs met.

"I have compassion for these people; they have already been with Me three days and have nothing to eat. I do not want to send them away hungry, or they may collapse on the way."

Matthew 15:32

LIVING IT

Have you ever wondered how the words in this verse can be true since there are some places in the world where people don't have enough food and water? Good question. The thing is, God's people have a responsibility to take care of some parts of God's work. There are many organizations that do their best to supply food and water to hungry people around the world. But, they need money and workers to do so. So, while God can certainly provide food in miraculous ways, He also expects His people to do their part to help others around the world.

August 6

> "Get behind Me, Satan! You are a stumbling block to Me; you do not have in mind the things of God, but the things of men."
> Matthew 16:23

Wow, these are powerful words. Especially when you consider that Jesus said them to His friend, Peter!

Jesus had just predicted His own death, which was a big part of the reason that He came to earth. Peter's response was, "No way! That won't happen."

Jesus knew His purpose for coming to earth and He followed that purpose. He couldn't let anyone stand in the way – not Peter – not you – not anyone!

LIVING IT

Have you ever thought about how you would have responded if you lived in the time Jesus was on earth and heard Him say that He was going to die soon? Would you have said the same thing Peter did? Or, would you have humbly thanked Jesus for sacrificing His own life? Well, how do you respond to Jesus' sacrifice now?

Your words and actions show whether you are truly grateful. If you take Jesus' death lightly and act like it's no big deal, then He may say these same words to you. Keep the things of God in your mind – His plan for all people to come to know Him.

FOLLOW JESUS

> "If anyone would come after Me, he must deny himself and take up his cross and follow Me."
>
> Matthew 16:24

Jesus had just told His disciples that He was going to die. That must have been a scary thing for them to hear. Maybe they wondered if their lives were in danger, too, since they were close followers of His.

Jesus wanted His followers to know that they must put aside any fear of suffering or pain. That is important for you, too.

It's hard to fully serve Jesus if you are afraid of something. So focus on God's plan and how you can be a part of it and follow Him – no matter what.

LIVING IT

Nathan is a Christian. One of his teachers does not believe in God and makes fun of anyone who is a Christian, especially students. He singles them out and asks them questions that he knows will challenge their faith. If their answers mention God he really goes off on them. As Nathan listens to him rant and rave about how ridiculous Christianity is he knows that he could just be quiet. Or, he could respectfully tell this teacher that God is a very real presence in his life. Scary? Yes, but sometimes that's what it means to take up your cross to follow Jesus.

August 8

> "What good will it be for a man if he gains the whole world, yet forfeits his soul? Or what can a man give in exchange for his soul?"
> Matthew 16:26

Some people have big dreams of what they want to accomplish in life.

Many dream of being rich beyond belief. Some dream of fame and recognition. Others want to be at the top of their chosen careers.

These are all fine dreams, but according to Jesus, if you accomplish any of these things but don't take care of your soul by accepting Jesus and living for Him, none of it is any good.

Deal with the really important thing first – your relationship with God.

LIVING IT

Stephen has big dreams. He loves science and plans to be a research doctor one day. He dreams of discovering cures for serious diseases. Stephen puts all his energy into studying and reading about science. He hopes that someday one of his discoveries will be named after him so that he will be famous forever. These are good dreams but Stephen has not even thought about Jesus and the gift of salvation He offers. Stephen may become a great doctor and do wonderful things some-day, but that won't get him into heaven – only accepting Jesus will do that.

MAKE CHANGES NOW

"The Son of Man is going to come in His Father's glory with His angels, and then He will reward each person according to what he has done."
Matthew 16:27

Jesus promised His followers that one day He will come back to earth and take His followers to heaven with Him.

That will be an amazing day! It will also be a day of answering for how you have lived your life. Jesus will reward you for your obedience to Him.

There will be no hiding any of the times you were disobedient and no way to change any of it. Changes in how you live can only be made now.

LIVING IT

Sammy is selfish. He does what he wants to do. He doesn't pay any attention to the Bible or how Jesus wants him to live, even though his parents take him to church and try to model a good Christian life. Sometimes he is mean to other kids and has even been known to tell lies to keep himself out of trouble. One day Sammy will have to answer for his behavior. He will answer to Jesus and there will be no way to change his past then. The best thing to do is to change now – accept Jesus as Savior and start living for Him, Sammy!

August 10

> "If you have faith as small as a mustard seed, you can say to this mountain, 'Move from here to there,' and it will move. Nothing will be impossible for you."
>
> Matthew 17:20

People tend to believe in what they can see. Things that must be taken simply by faith are harder for us. But because God's kingdom is a spiritual kingdom, much of it must be taken by faith.

Jesus encourages that faith by telling us that we can do amazing things if we just have faith. Think about the miracles Jesus did while He was on earth; healings, raising dead people back to life and returning to life Himself.

God's power is available to us, too if we have even a tiny bit of faith.

LIVING IT

How cool would it be to be able to move a mountain from one spot to another just by thinking it or praying for it to move? OK, that might not be something you actually need to do. But, how about having enough faith to do miracles that really help people like Jesus did?

There is an amazing amount of power available to Jesus' followers – power to do His work in the world and to help people in wonderful ways. A mustard seed is a teeny tiny seed and just that little bit of faith can make a difference. Awesome!

August 11

CHILDLIKE HUMILITY

> "Whoever humbles himself like this child is the greatest in the kingdom of heaven."
> Matthew 18:4

The opposite of pride is humility. Pride is all about self. It's a "Yay me!" kind of attitude. Humility is about others.

A humble person thinks about others first and cares about what happens to them. Jesus says that a humble attitude is the winner in His kingdom.

Children are so good at caring about others. They haven't learned the drive to be number one so they often care about the needs of others. Jesus says to strive for that childlike kind of attitude that trusts Him, wants to please Him and wants to help others.

LIVING IT

Tanner's neighbor, Mrs. Olson, has a dog that is her only family. She loves that dog. Duke isn't a big dog but he's not small either. Tanner often sees Mrs. Olson walking Duke during the day. She is not very strong and Duke kind of drags her around. Tanner is afraid of Duke and even a little afraid of Mrs. Olson, who can be kind of crabby. One day Tanner saw Duke jerk his leash so hard that Mrs. Olson nearly fell. Tanner decided to get over his fear. He went over and offered to walk Duke. Tanner put Mrs. Olson and Duke ahead of his fears and that humility pleases Jesus.

August 12

> "How hard it is for the rich to enter the kingdom of God!"
> Mark 10:23

People with a lot of money can buy whatever they need, so they sometimes do not need to be dependent on anyone – not even God.

A healthy relationship with God is one that is submissive to Him and recognizes Him as the authority over all things – even money.

Jesus taught that money and material possessions should be generously shared with others. The rich man Jesus was speaking with here would not do that.

Holding too tightly onto material possessions makes it hard to serve God.

LIVING IT

Terrell is basically homeless. He and his mom stay at a city shelter to have a place to sleep. Terrell wants to go to school more than just about any boy ever has, but he doesn't have decent clothes or money for supplies or to pay the school fees.

Well, he didn't have the money, but someone has "adopted" him and now pays for everything he needs for school, even the fees so he can be on a sports team. In Terrell's mind, that person is a true Christian because he shares what he has instead of holding on to money tightly.

GIVE UP WORRY

"All things are possible with God."
Mark 10:27

Think about this: Jesus says that anything is possible with God.

When He said this He was responding to a question from His disciples about who could possibly be saved if rich people couldn't.

But the point is not whether rich or poor is better, the point is that God can do anything – save anyone – help anyone – change anything. God is God and nothing is impossible for Him!

LIVING IT

Is there some problem occupying your mind and heart right now? Do you think it is impossible to solve? Do you think it's unlikely that it will be settled in a way that makes you happy? In other words, are you giving up?

Wait! Don't give up. Give it to God instead. His power, strength and love for you are greater than you can even imagine. All things are possible for Him. If He doesn't change the situation, He will change your desires. He will handle it in the way that is best for everybody concerned! Trust Him.

August 14

A GREAT SERVANT

"Whoever wants to become great among you must be your servant, and whoever wants to be first must be slave of all."

Mark 10:43-44

To the world this is upside down thinking. Who would choose to be a servant or a slave? Most guys dream of being their own boss so they can be in control over others. So why would Jesus say this?

Well, remember that Jesus is all about relationships and loving others. He encourages His followers to put the needs of others before their own.

Be a servant to others instead of thinking only of your own desires.

LIVING IT

Carsen wants to be a leader so that other guys will follow him. He wants the power that it will give him.

Harris doesn't really care about being popular or having others follow him. But, he does care about other kids and looks for ways to help others in any way he can. Harris especially notices kids who are usually left out of things. He tries to talk to those guys and be friends with them. Harris will end up with lots of friends who think he is very special.

GOD'S SALT

"Salt is good, but if it loses its saltiness, how can you make it salty again? Have salt in yourselves, and be at peace with each other."

Mark 9:50

Once you get used to the taste of salt on your food, anything that isn't salty tastes a little bit boring. Salt adds flavor and takes the boring away.

Jesus said that His followers are like salt in the world because they add flavor and take the boring away. The flavor that Christians add is the taste of God's love and mercy.

His love is deeper and stronger than anything and it is the believer's job to share it with the world.

LIVING IT

All the guys know that Dallas is a Christian. He is very open about his faith. Sometimes a group of guys is hanging out and talking and laughing. But when Dallas walks up, they suddenly stop talking. It's not that they aren't friendly. It's just that they aren't comfortable with what their conversation is about when he comes around. It is good that Dallas makes them uncomfortable. Because he is a Christian his friends feel weird about some of the jokes they tell and some of the things they say when he is around. Dallas is God's salt to the world around him.

August 16

SERVING OTHERS

"For even the Son of Man did not come to be served, but to serve, and to give His life as a ransom for many."

Mark 10:45

Jesus called for His followers to serve others by putting others' needs and desires ahead of their own. That's not always an easy thing to do.

But, Jesus doesn't ask His followers to do anything that He doesn't do Himself. Jesus served others by giving His time and energy to teach, heal the sick, and even raise dead people back to life.

Jesus didn't just do what He wanted to do with His time. He gave His time, energy and even His life for others.

LIVING IT

How can you serve others as consistently as Jesus did? Does it seem like it would get tiring to always be looking for things to do for others?

Start by asking God to open your eyes to ways to serve others. Then be willing to act on what He shows you. He may show you simple, small ways to be kind or helpful.

As you obey those things, He will show you bigger ways you can serve. Just do what He asks you to do.

TRUE FAITH

> "Have faith in God."
> Mark 11:22

It sounds so simple, doesn't it – just have faith in God. But, what does it mean to have faith in God?

Faith means believing in God's power, strength and love. It means trusting Him to take care of you and to always do what is best for you. It means completely giving yourself over to Him because you know He is in control of absolutely everything.

God loves you more than you can possibly imagine. Have faith in God. His power is available to you to do incredible things for Him.

LIVING IT

Jason loudly proclaims, "I believe in God. He's awesome!" But, there isn't much evidence of that in his life. What does a lack of faith look like? Well, Jason worries about pretty much everything and not just a little bit of worry, but worry that sucks the life right out of him.

When he prays it feels like his prayers bounce off the ceiling right back at him. Why? Because he doesn't really, honestly believe – he doesn't have faith in God. Jason doesn't believe in God's love, strength or power.

August 18

THE POWER OF PRAYER

"Whatever you ask for in prayer, believe that you have received it, and it will be yours."
Mark 11:24

Do you really believe that God hears your prayers and that He will answer them?

Prayer is your opportunity to tell Him what's on your heart. Of course it is important to pray in God's will.

What does that mean? Just that it is important to read His Word and make every effort to obey and serve Him. Then, the things you pray for will more likely be things that are good for you.

Just know that, as Jesus says, He will hear your prayers, and yes, He will answer them.

LIVING IT

Terry read this verse and thought, *Cool. I can get an "A" on my math test and I can get a new scooter and I can get ...* Yeah, he doesn't get it. God is not a big Santa Claus in the sky who will give you anything you want or do stuff so that you don't have to do your work.

Yes, He wants you to tell Him things you are concerned about. Sometimes His answer may be comfort for you instead of changing the situation. He wants to hear what you think you need. But most importantly, He wants to give you what is best for you.

August 19

BE HONEST

"Watch out for the teachers of the law. They like to walk around in flowing robes and be greeted in the marketplaces, and have the most important seats in the synagogues and the places of honor at banquets."

Mark 12:38-39

Does this seem like a strange warning from Jesus? After all, the teachers of the law were the religious experts of the time so it might seem like they would be the ones whom people should respect and obey. Not really – because Jesus questioned their motives.

The Pharisees liked to be noticed and felt that they were more important than other people. Remember, Jesus sees what's in a person's heart so He knows why people do what they do.

These teachers might fool other people, but Jesus sees that their hearts are full of pride, not love for others.

LIVING IT

Andrew thinks he is something special. He quotes Bible verses and is the first one to volunteer to pray in Sunday school class. It looks like Andrew is a devoted Christian. But what no one knows is that when he is alone he doesn't pray or read his Bible.

His heart is not devoted to God. He just wants everyone to think that he is. Andrew wants the praise of people without being close to God. He may fool the people around him, but he doesn't fool God because He can see Andrew's heart.

August 20

> "Be on your guard; I have told you everything ahead of time."
> Mark 13:23

Things should be easy when you have complete instructions, right?

Everything you need to know about living for God is in the Bible. Jesus gave instructions and challenges to keep you on track.

He also gave warnings that there are people who will try to pull you away from serving God. They make up their own rules and try to get others to live by them. They follow their own version of what the Bible teaches.

Jesus said to be on the lookout for people who try to pull you away from the truth. Know what He teaches – know the Bible and you will be just fine.

LIVING IT

Some guys think the Bible is kind of hard to understand. It's true – some of it is. So, how can you know it well enough to protect yourself and to "be on your guard?" If you read something you don't understand, ask someone you trust what it means. There are also some versions of the Bible that are easier to understand.

Remember that God wants you to understand the Bible, so ask Him to help you understand His Word. Keep reading and you will keep learning. Be careful about listening to someone who teaches something you know goes against the Bible.

FUTURE HOPE

This is so awesome! Jesus is coming back someday!

He promises to come back to earth in great power and glory and get His children and take them to heaven with Him!

Whatever problems you face in life will one day be history as you join Jesus in the glory of heaven forever!

Jesus promises to come from heaven and take you there with Him!

> "At that time men will see the Son of Man coming in clouds with great power and glory. And He will send His angels and gather His elect from the four winds, from the ends of the earth to the ends of the heavens."
>
> Mark 13:26-27

LIVING IT

Rick doesn't have a lot of hope that life will ever get better. Life has been a struggle for him since day one. He has some learning problems so school is no fun. His parents are always short on money. Rick doesn't have many friends. He wonders if life will ever be easier.

This promise from Jesus makes Rick feel better, because he knows that one day everything will be better because he will be with Jesus and everything in heaven will be good!

> "Therefore keep watch because you do not know when the owner of the house will come back – whether in the evening, or at midnight, or when the rooster crows, or at dawn. If He comes suddenly, do not let Him find you sleeping."
>
> Mark 13:35-36

Hey – pay attention! Jesus warns His followers to pay constant attention to how they are living because no one knows exactly when He will return to earth to get His followers and take them to heaven.

Some people claim that they know when Jesus is returning, but they don't really know. The Bible says that no one knows.

So, don't get lazy about obeying Jesus. Be careful to constantly live for Him and be obedient to Him. Then, you will be ready when He comes!

LIVING IT

George has grown up going to church. He knows all about the Bible and salvation. He figures that some day he will accept Jesus and live for Him. Someday. Right now he wants to do whatever he wants and just have fun. George figures he has time to accept Jesus when he is older, but Jesus warns against that attitude!

George must realize that no one knows when Jesus is coming back, so putting off accepting Him as Savior is taking a chance. Besides, George can enjoy life now even more with Jesus as his Savior!

August 23

WORSHIP FIRST

> "The poor you will always have with you, and you can help them any time you want. But you will not always have Me."
>
> Mark 14:7

A woman poured some very expensive perfume on Jesus as she worshiped Him.

Some people complained that she was wasting the valuable perfume. They thought it should be sold and the money given to the poor. At least that's what they said.

Jesus stopped their complaints though by pointing out that the woman was worshiping Him, which was more than they were doing.

There will always be poor people to help. She worshiped Jesus while He was right there with her.

LIVING IT

It's always good to help the poor. In fact, Jesus often said that His followers should share what they had with others. He said to help people who are poor, lonely or sick. But the act of helping others should never be more important than worshiping Jesus.

Take time to be alone with Jesus and worship Him with no distractions from other things – even good things. Then help others as He tells you to do.

August 24

> "Put out into deep water and let down the nets for a catch."
>
> Luke 5:4

Jesus said this to some fishermen who had already been out fishing all night, but had caught nothing.

Peter (who became one of Jesus' followers) wanted to argue with Jesus, but he didn't. Peter did what Jesus asked and the result was a catch of fish so big that they could barely pull the nets in.

Jesus blessed Peter beyond his wildest dreams because Peter believed Him and did what He asked.

LIVING IT

How courageous are you? Are you willing to take a chance? If Jesus asked you to do something that seemed impossible or hopeless, would you give it a try?

Sometimes the things Jesus asks seem a bit scary or even kind of strange because you can't see the big picture like He does. Just like Peter, you may be blessed beyond your wildest dreams when you choose to do what Jesus asks!

August 25

MAKING A WAY

> "I have not come to call the righteous, but sinners to repentance."
>
> Luke 5:32

Jesus came to earth to help people who needed Him.

God's plan from the minute Adam and Eve sinned was for Jesus to make a way for people to have a personal relationship with Him and to be forgiven of their sins.

He wanted people to come face to face with their sin, then turn away from it and be able to join Him in heaven some day. That's why Jesus came to call sinners.

LIVING IT

Does this somehow seem to not relate to you? Who are the sinners Jesus came for? You. Actually every person who lives. The Bible says that every single person is a sinner. So, Jesus came to call everyone to repentance. That means you need to recognize that you are a sinner (that means you disobey God's laws, are selfish, hurtful toward others). Confess your sin to Jesus, ask His forgiveness, and invite Him into your heart to be your Savior. There, now Jesus has called you to repentance. Cool, huh?

August 26

> "Everyone who asks receives; he who seeks finds; and to him who knocks, the door will be opened."
>
> Luke 11:10

The most amazing gift from God is the Holy Spirit who lives in your heart. He guides your thoughts, actions and prayers.

So, as Jesus taught, when you want to know God and ask for His help in your life, the Holy Spirit will guide your prayers. That means your prayers will be answered and your understanding of God's work in your life will be deeper.

The more you ask, the more you learn. The more you learn, the more you know.

LIVING IT

"Please God, please, please," Ryan prayed. He just kept praying the same sentence over and over. He couldn't think of anything else to say. But, does God know what Ryan is asking Him to do? Does He know what Ryan is praying about?

Yep. Ryan has asked Jesus to be his Savior. He has God's Holy Spirit living in his heart. He tries to be obedient to Jesus' teachings and pay attention to the Holy Spirit's guidance in his prayers. Ryan loves God and he knows that God loves him.

August 27

THE HARDEST PLACE TO WITNESS

> "I tell you the truth, no prophet is accepted in his hometown."
>
> Luke 4:24

It must have made Jesus sad. The people who knew Him best – the ones who watched Him grow from childhood to manhood were the least likely to believe that He was God's true Son.

He wanted people to know that it is most difficult to convince those closest to you because they know you the best. In Jesus' case, of course, there was nothing bad they could say about Him. Maybe He was just too familiar.

This is a good reminder for you, however, that the people you care about the most may be the most doubtful about the realness of your relationship with Christ.

LIVING IT

Bryan is a new Christian and he is excited about his faith. He wants to tell everyone about Jesus. No one else in his family is a Christian and they don't want to hear anything about Bryan's faith. They say stuff like, "You're just showing off. We know the real you who throws fits and is selfish and mean to your brother." Bryan knows it's going to take a while for them to see that his heart has changed. But, he will keep living his faith in front of them. He will keep loving them. He will show them the new Bryan!

August 28

"Father, everything is possible for You. Take this cup from Me. Yet not what I will, but what You will."

Mark 14:36

Jesus prayed this prayer in the Garden of Gethsemane.

He knew what was coming for Him and it wasn't going to be pleasant. He would be tortured and eventually killed. It was an important part of God's plan that would make salvation possible for people.

Jesus was willing to do what God wanted. He submitted to God and trusted Him and loved you enough to do what God asked Him to do.

LIVING IT

Doing hard things is hard. Jeff knows that better than anyone because he isn't brave at all. He will usually try to find the easy way out of difficult things – from school projects to chores to obeying God.

But, when Jeff reads these words it makes him feel strong enough to do the right thing, even when it's hard. "Not My will, but Yours," he reads. If that's good enough for Jesus, then it's good enough for Jeff! He will try to do hard things – with Jesus' help!

August 29

WATCH AND PRAY!

> "Watch and pray so that you will not fall into temptation. The spirit is willing, but the body is weak."
>
> Mark 14:38

Jesus was in the Garden of Gethsemane and about to be arrested. Some of His friends were with Him.

He had asked them to watch and pray with Him. They must have seen how stressed He was, but they kept falling asleep instead of praying. They weren't focused on Him so they couldn't stay awake to help Him.

That's why Jesus gave this warning – stay focused. Watch and pray because if you aren't focused, then no matter how hard you try not to you will fall into temptation. Satan takes big advantage of that temptation.

LIVING IT

Will has a couple of friends who get into lots of trouble because of bad choices they make. Will likes to hang out with them because they are tons of fun and he thinks he can resist doing the things that get them into trouble.

But, he gets caught up in the fun and before he knows it he's in trouble, too. Just as Jesus said, Will's spirit wanted to stay out of trouble and obey Jesus, but his flesh was weak. Bummer.

"My Father, who has given them to Me, is greater than all; no one can snatch them out of My Father's hand."

John 10:29

What comfort there is in this verse. Jesus is letting everyone know that once you accept Him as Savior, you belong to Him and no one can ever change that.

God is greater and stronger than anyone or anything and that power protects you.

Yes, there will be temptations and yes, there will be problems, but hold firm to Jesus during all of them because He is holding firm to you!

LIVING IT

Beau and his family often vacation at the beach. One time when they were there a powerful storm blew in off the ocean. The wind pounded their hotel building. Trees were bent all the way to the ground by the powerful storm. Giant waves crashed onto the beach. Beau was frightened about what was going to happen.

But even in that storm he knew that God was holding tightly to him. Nothing could pull him away from God's love. He is protecting Beau, taking care of him and watching over him. Beau belongs to God.

August 31

Stick close to Jesus. That's where your strength comes from. Jesus explains this by using the example of a vine.

The branches of the vine get their food and water by staying connected to the vine. It's impossible for a branch to get its own nutrition and be able to grow fruit. That only happens by staying connected to the vine.

The same is true for Christians. You must stay connected to Jesus who gives you spiritual food and strength. He helps you grow fruit for Him!

> "Remain in Me and I will remain in you. No branch can bear fruit by itself; it must remain in the vine. Neither can you bear fruit unless you remain in Me."
>
> John 15:4

LIVING IT

How do you "remain" in Jesus? What does that mean? It means to stay connected to Him by reading His Word. This teaches you how to obey Him and live for Him. You also stay connected by praying – talking with Him and then just by being quiet sometimes so that He can speak with you.

Only by staying connected to Jesus can you effectively grow fruit for Him. What is fruit for Jesus? It's sharing His love with others and living for Him.

September 1

USEFUL LIVES

> "If anyone does not remain in Me, he is like a branch that is thrown away and withers; such branches are picked up, thrown into the fire and burned."
>
> John 15:6

Following Jesus is serious business. Yes, He loves you, but He warns against taking living for Him lightly.

Jesus encourages you to stay close to Him so you can get your strength from Him. If you don't get strength from Him, you are pretty much useless – like a dead branch that is cut off a tree and thrown away because it has no use.

To avoid being useless, stay close to Jesus.

LIVING IT

Jesus doesn't walk away from those who don't stay close to Him. He patiently waits for them to come back.

But what a lot of time is wasted when you don't stay close to Him. Time that could be spent learning more about Him and serving Him and encouraging others to get to know Him, too! Stay close to Jesus and learn and grow.

September 2

> "As the Father has loved Me, so have I loved you. Now remain in My love."
> John 15:9

God loves you the way He loves His Son and God loves Jesus very much.

His love is complete, sacrificial, and never stops giving. You know what's amazing? Jesus loves you in the very same way! Isn't that amazing?

He loves you completely, and of course, sacrificially. His love asks for nothing in return except that you love Him back and stick close to Him.

What an amazing gift – to be loved by Jesus.

LIVING IT

Marc loves the way this verse makes him feel! Jesus loves him! And He loves Marc more than he can even imagine! What a great thing to know. When he is feeling lonely or sad, he remembers that Jesus loves him! When he feels happy and wants to celebrate, he remembers that Jesus loves him!

Marc is so happy to remember that Jesus loves him that he loves reading the Bible and thinking about Him and even singing about Him. Marc sticks close to Jesus because he knows Jesus loves him!

September 3

TRUE JOY

> "I have told you this so that My joy may be in you and that your joy may be complete."
>
> John 15:11

Jesus wants you to know that the things He teaches in the Bible are not meant to make your life unhappy. They are not a bunch of rules that you have to keep.

Jesus taught the things in the Bible knowing that if you live the way He teaches, you will be filled with joy! Your relationship with God will be good and your relationships with other people will be good as well because you will treat them with respect.

Follow Jesus and be filled with complete joy!

LIVING IT

What's the deal with joy? No one is happy all the time, right? Well, joy and happiness are not the same thing. Joy comes from deep down inside and keeps you going even when you aren't happy.

Landon has noticed that the closer he follows Jesus, the more joy he has. There are times when Landon is not happy because of problems or bad moods. But even when he isn't happy, he has an underlying joy because he knows that Jesus loves him and that He is guiding and protecting him.

September 4

LOVE ONE ANOTHER

"My command is this: Love each other as I have loved you."
John 15:12

Jesus is all about love. He encourages His followers to love others – not just their friends but everyone. Just love.

The love that Jesus shows by His example is unselfish and sacrificial. He holds nothing back from those He loves.

Now Jesus commands you to love in the same way He loves. It isn't always easy to love this way, but you don't have to do it on your own. Jesus helps you to love others in ways you never knew you could.

LIVING IT

OK, Tim doesn't talk about love. It sounds kind of mushy. But he does love his family and his friends. In fact he loves most people. But there is one person he has a little trouble with: Tony.

He tries to love Tony, but Tony is mean. It's hard for Tim to even want nice things to happen for Tony. So, Tim asks God to help him love this difficult friend. Guess what? God does help him! He helps him love Tony in the same way God loves him!

PROOF FOR DOUBTERS

> "Don't tell anyone, but go, show yourself to the priest and offer the sacrifices that Moses commanded for your cleansing, as a testimony to them."
>
> Luke 5:14

Jesus knew that the hardest people to convince that He was truly the Messiah – the Son of God – were the religious people.

So, when He healed a man who had leprosy – a terrible skin disease – He told the man to keep quiet about it until he had told the priest and offered the sacrifices that were required.

He wanted the man to do everything by the book so that the priest would have to admit that a miracle had taken place and that Jesus was the reason.

LIVING IT

People who *think* they have all the answers are the hardest people to convince that they *may not* have all the answers. Dawson has seen this first-hand. His older brother thinks he knows pretty much everything and he has no place in his life for God. In fact, he's bitter against God though no one knows why. So, Dawson takes every opportunity to give credit to God when he can and prays that his faithfulness to God will be noticed by his brother. He is a testimony to his brother of God's work in his life.

September 6

"Do not judge, and you will not be judged. Do not condemn, and you will not be condemned. Forgive, and you will be forgiven."

Luke 6:37

Treat other people the way you want to be treated. That's not so hard, is it?

Well, it shouldn't be, but unfortunately it sometimes is. Jesus made a point (a couple of times) that it's important to treat other people the way you want to be treated, even by God.

Why should you expect God to forgive you if you can't treat other people in that same manner?

Think about how you treat others because it matters.

LIVING IT

This verse kind of gets under Zach's skin. Like, he can't stop thinking about it. Because Zach is a Christian whenever he asks God to forgive his sins, the first thing that comes to mind is a friend he has been holding a grudge against.

A grudge – yeah, Zach refuses to forgive this guy for something he did to him – something that really isn't a big deal when he thinks about it. Yeah, that's God reminding Zach to forgive others before he asks God to forgive him. That's how it works.

FOLLOW THE LEADER?

"Can a blind man lead a blind man? Will they not both fall into a pit?"

Luke 6:39

Jesus often warned people to be careful about whom they were listening to and whom they were following. Why? Because if you listen to someone who doesn't really know any more than you know (even if he acts like he does) then you aren't going to get good guidance and help.

Yep, it would be like a blind man leading a blind man across a busy eight-lane highway ... gulp.

Choose the wisest, most loving person to follow – Jesus.

LIVING IT

Michael has pushed himself into being the guy who lots of other guys follow. If he accepts a new guy into the group, so do the others. If he says something is cool to do, the others think so, too.

The problem with this is that Michael doesn't follow Jesus' teachings. He doesn't care about God at all. So, he leads people away from God. He's not the best guy to follow!

September 8

> "Why do you look at the speck of sawdust in your brother's eye and pay no attention to the plank in your own eye?"
> Luke 6:41

It is so easy to criticize others – especially when a group of guys get together and start picking on someone. Jesus raises the question of why this happens.

After all, no one is perfect. Every single person is a sinner. So, why judge someone for some small fault you see when you have huge problems with your own behavior?

Seriously, it's probably true that whatever bugs you in another kid's behavior is a problem because it's something you struggle with, too – big time!

LIVING IT

"Dude! You are so lazy! Just go get me a dish of ice cream, will you?" Chris said. His brother, Glenn, just shook his head. "You're calling me lazy because I won't go to the kitchen for you? You're just stretched out on the couch. You're the lazy one."

OK, name calling isn't the answer, but Glenn is right – Chris is criticizing him for something that Chris is guilty of, too. The message is, "Take care of your own problems before you criticize someone else!"

September 9

TOTAL SHARING

"Give to everyone who asks you, and if anyone takes what belongs to you, do not demand it back."

Luke 6:30

Complete unselfishness is what Jesus requests of His followers.

He encourages you to be so focused on helping others that you do not hold anything back from sharing with them. Jesus wants His followers to be so aware of people's needs that, should someone take something that belongs to you because they really need it, you do not ask for it back.

If Jesus had His way, no one would go hungry and no one would be homeless because those who have enough food and money would share with the poor.

LIVING IT

Lincoln wants to understand Jesus' call to be totally unselfish. It isn't easy to always notice other people's needs, but he prays for Jesus' help to have an attitude of generosity. Lincoln does really care about others.

When he hears of people who don't have enough food or water or children who don't have any toys or books, he wants to help. Lincoln is even willing to give away his own stuff – even new stuff. He always has more than he needs so why not share with others? It's the Jesus thing to do!

September 10

WHAT'S INSIDE COUNTS

"No good tree bears bad fruit, nor does a bad tree bear good fruit."
Luke 6:43

Everyone makes bad choices sometimes. Everyone makes mistakes. But, a boy who has asked Jesus to be his Savior has the love of Jesus in his heart.

In this example from Jesus, that boy would be a good tree and he would bear good fruit. That means he would love God and others. People would be able to see that Jesus is in his heart by the way he lives – the evidence in his life.

LIVING IT

Kerry knows what good fruit from a good tree looks like. His grandmother is the kindest, most loving person Kerry has ever met. Grandma always says that God has done so much for her that His love just overflows from her heart and spills out to others.

She is an amazing example to Kerry of sharing God's love with others through her kindness and generosity. She gives her time, her energy, cooks food for others, drives them places. She just helps in any way she can!

September 11

GET RID OF THE JUNK

"He cuts off every branch in Me that bears no fruit, while every branch that does bear fruit He prunes so that it will be even more fruitful."

John 15:2

News flash! Life will not be problem-free just because you ask Jesus to be your Savior. In fact, sometimes you may feel like you have more than your share of problems.

Jesus actually promises that some of the difficult times will be to help you grow in your relationship with Him.

Does that sound hard? Yes, it may be difficult some-times, but stay focused on what you can learn from Jesus through the difficulties.

LIVING IT

Brett doesn't get it. Does this verse mean that God is going to send bad things into his life? That's not the best way to look at this verse. God may allow things to happen that will make Brett choose whether to follow Him or not. Making those choices help Brett realize whether or not his heart is focused on God. It will help him grow. Just as a gardener cuts off dead branches from a tree, the choices Brett learns to make will cut dead areas out of his life. He will come out stronger after the problems are settled.

September 12

> "If you obey My commands, you will remain in My love, just as I have obeyed My Father's commands and remain in His love."
>
> John 15:10

God's love for you is free, but it comes with a challenge that you return His love and make every effort to obey Him.

Deliberately disobeying God breaks your relationship with Him.

Jesus is your example. He obeyed God even when it was difficult. But, because He obeyed He knew that He and God were close and that He could rest in God's love.

LIVING IT

Being obedient is definitely not always easy. A lot of things in the world and many people around you will encourage you not to obey God. They tell you being obedient is just living by a bunch of rules.

What they don't know is that obeying God is proof that you love God and are working on learning to love Him even more. The more you love Him the more you know you can depend on Him. He loves you even more than you love Him and He will take care of you – always.

September 13

THE GREATEST LOVE EXAMPLE

> "Greater love has no one than this, that he lay down his life for his friends."
> John 15:13

Jesus showed His love for you in a way that is unlike anyone else!

He said that the greatest evidence of someone's love for you would be if he is willing to give his own life. Jesus did.

He died for you so that you can be set free of your sins, but He also dedicated His life on earth to teaching and loving you!

LIVING IT

OK, does this mean that you need to physically die to show that you love your friends? No, of course not. So how do you lay down your life for a friend? It's a day in and day out thing. You take all selfishness and self-centeredness out of your life and dedicate yourself to serving and helping others in any way you can.

Make others your focus – not yourself. You have a great example to follow – Jesus focused His daily life to teaching, loving and helping others. Follow His example!

September 14

REAL FRIENDSHIP

> "I no longer call you servants, because a servant does not know his master's business. Instead, I have called you friends, for everything that I learned from My Father I have made known to you."
>
> John 15:15

Look at the relationship described in this statement.

Jesus takes your relationship with Him from the master-servant level to the level of friendship.

What does that mean? A servant only knows information that his master chooses to share with him. A servant does what he is told to do. He takes orders from his master.

A friend knows personal information. A friend is an equal. Jesus wants a close relationship with you – a friendship.

LIVING IT

Kevin's friends are very important to him. He has really good friends so he knows what a healthy friendship is like even if he doesn't think about the health of his relationships very much.

When Kevin reads that Jesus calls him a friend, Kevin gets really excited. It's much easier to love a friend than it is to love a master. He is very thankful that Jesus is his friend and that He shares everything God has taught Him with Kevin. This is real friendship!

September 15

SIMPLICITY

So, maybe you aren't really into clothes. As long as you have clothes to wear, do you not really care what they look like? Well, then what do these verses mean?

They mean that God will take care of you. He will make sure you have whatever you need.

Don't get confused. What you need is not the same as what you want. These words are a reminder that you can trust God to provide what you need.

> "Why do you worry about clothes? See how the lilies of the field grow. They do not labor or spin. Yet I tell you that not even Solomon in all his splendor was dressed like one of these."
>
> Matthew 6:28-29

LIVING IT

What you need versus what you want. That's the important difference here. You may not feel that God always gives you things you think you need. But, He knows the difference between what you need and what you want.

How does this fit with people who don't have the food they need or a home to live in? Yes, it's hard to understand, but sometimes God provides the comfort or peace you need to get through a situation rather than changing the situation.

"Watch out for
false prophets.
They come to
you in sheep's
clothing, but
inwardly they
are ferocious
wolves."
Matthew 7:15

Be careful. Be careful. Be careful about listening to people who teach things that don't agree with what Jesus teaches.

Some people think they know the right way to live or to know God, but if you look at how they live and how they treat other people you see that their lives do not reflect Jesus or His love.

Often they have taken only parts of Jesus' teaching to obey instead of all the teachings in the Bible.

LIVING IT

From the time Jaden asked Jesus into his heart, his parents have encouraged him to read his Bible every day. They got him a Bible that is easy to understand and they have a family Bible study time, too. Here they can answer questions about anything Jaden doesn't understand.

They believe it is important to know God's Word because it is absolute truth. The Word of God guards their hearts against false teachers – even those who make their way sound wonderfully appealing. Truth is the best way!

September 17

GOOD THOUGHTS

"Why do you entertain evil thoughts in your hearts?"
Matthew 9:4

Jesus was speaking to some religious teachers who were criticizing some of the stuff He did.

It's pretty sad because these guys were so focused on living by rules instead of loving people. Since their hearts were not filled with love all they could think about was that they wanted Jesus and others to obey their rules.

Since they didn't listen to Jesus, their hearts were judgmental and critical.

LIVING IT

Andrew is unhappy and angry and frustrated. He is so angry, but sometimes doesn't even know why. A big part of his problem is that most of the time he only thinks about himself and how everything affects him. When others don't pay enough attention to him then he has bad thoughts about them.

The sad thing is that Andrew knows he should let Jesus fill his heart with love for others and stop thinking about himself so much. He needs to put good thoughts in his mind.

September 18

> "Whoever acknowledges Me before men, I will also acknowledge him before My Father in heaven."
>
> Matthew 10:32

There is no such thing as a secret Christian. It is a Christian's responsibility to share the love of God with other people – so that all people everywhere can hear of His love.

The openness of your faith, which spills out of a heart devoted to God, shows God's love to others. Jesus honors this faith by acknowledging you to God as one of His own.

LIVING IT

Luke is super shy. He is so shy that he has trouble even talking to anyone who isn't a friend. So the idea of telling someone about his faith in Jesus makes him sick to his stomach.

But Luke is amazed to find out that it really isn't so hard. He takes a minute to say a silent thank you prayer at lunch. That shows his faith. He mentions to a friend that he goes to church and that shares his faith. It's a step-by-step acknowledgment of his faith. Then, one day a friend asks him more about it and Luke can tell him how much Jesus means to him!

September 19

THE SPIRIT LEADS

> "The Counselor, the Holy Spirit, whom the Father will send in My name, will teach you all things and will remind you of everything I have said to you."
>
> John 14:26

When Jesus was ready to go back to heaven He promised that God would send the Holy Spirit to live in believers' hearts and be with them always and always. He did!

So, anytime you don't quite know if something is right or wrong, the Spirit will lead you.

Jesus promised that the Holy Spirit would help you remember all that Jesus taught. All you have to do is ask for His help, then listen to Him!

LIVING IT

Austin wonders how the Spirit leads. "He doesn't e-mail, text or write messages on the wall. So, how do I know when the Spirit is leading me?" Well, Austin, do you know that feeling you get sometimes when you are wondering if something you want to do is right or wrong? You know, there is a little voice in your mind that says, "Do this." Or, "Don't do this." If you're seeking God's guidance then there is a good chance that's the Spirit leading. Sometimes He even reminds you of Bible verses you have read that help you know right from wrong!

September 20

> "Come, follow Me," Jesus said, "and I will make you fishers of men."
>
> Matthew 4:19

Jesus called His disciples to follow Him and He promised that He would give them a new purpose in their lives. They would have the same purpose He had – to bring people to faith in Him.

Jesus' followers today still have that same purpose. As you follow Jesus He will show you how to lead others to faith in Him.

He used the fishing example in talking with His disciples because they were fishermen. Look for Him to use ways you are familiar with, also.

LIVING IT

Brian plays soccer. He is on two different teams so he spends a lot of time at practice and games. He has made some good friends on the teams.

Brian does not get in his friends' faces about sharing his faith. But he follows Jesus' instructions and looks for ways to gently share his faith, even just by the way he lives. His teammates notice his sportsmanship and kindness and all the ways he behaves with his soccer friends. They notice.

THINKING OF OTHERS

> "Blessed are the poor in spirit, for theirs is the kingdom of heaven."
> Matthew 5:3

Jesus knew that the world gives a lot of honor and authority to powerful, strong and wealthy people. He made it plain that none of those things are important to God.

He wasn't giving honor to poor people, but to those who are poor in spirit. That means humble people who show kindness, respect and honor to others over themselves. That is a spirit that reflects Jesus.

LIVING IT

Stanley felt sorry for children who have a parent in prison. He thought that must be hard on them. So, he started a program to do something nice for them. He collects winter hats, mittens and warm socks for these kids – with an occasional toy thrown in for fun. Some of Stan's friends joined in and the program grew. He has a gift for noticing people who are lonely or left out. But He doesn't just notice, he does something about it. Stanley thinks of others before himself and that makes God happy.

September 22

> "Rejoice and be glad, because great is your reward in heaven, for in the same way they persecuted the prophets who were before you."
>
> Matthew 5:12

Jesus knew that some people would be upset at the message that they are sinners. They would get angry at anyone who pointed it out and they would be mean to the one who delivered that message. Jesus knew this because it happened to Him.

The good news is right at the beginning of this statement – your reward is in heaven.

Jesus is paying attention. He knows what's happening and He will reward His faithful followers.

LIVING IT

Devin took his faith in Jesus seriously. So seriously that he sometimes refused to join in certain activities or conversations with his friends. Some of the kids made fun of him because of that. It hurt. He didn't think he was better than anyone else. He was just trying to be the best Devin he could be.

He kept right on living as he always had because he knew it was right and he knew that Jesus knew he was doing the right thing. That was good enough for him.

GO THE EXTRA MILE

> "If someone forces you to go one mile, go with him two miles."
> Matthew 5:41

There should be a noticeable difference between how a Christian treats others and how someone who doesn't know Christ treats others.

Jesus says His followers should go the extra mile. That means whatever a person asks of you, do that and even more.

Surprise people with your generosity, helpfulness and kindness. And make sure they know that it comes from a heart focused on loving and obeying Jesus.

LIVING IT

"Anyone who has time please stay after class and help stack up the chairs," Christopher's teacher said. When the bell rang all the students dashed out the door. But, Christopher stayed behind and began stacking chairs with the teacher. After a few minutes the teacher said, "Thanks for your help, Christopher, but you can go now. I'll finish. I know you're eager to get home." But Christopher didn't leave. He stayed until every chair was stacked. The teacher knows Christopher is a Christian and she sees evidence of that in Christopher's life.

September 24

NO STRINGS ATTACHED

> "Give to the one who asks you, and do not turn away from the one who wants to borrow from you."
> Matthew 5:42

A generous heart is an unselfish heart. Jesus encourages His followers to be generous to all people.

Don't hold on to your possessions as though they are more important to you than people are. Nothing is more important than people. So be generous to all, and do not worry about being repaid.

LIVING IT

September 25

Jared thinks he is a pretty generous person. He really is ... with his friends. But, when his little brother wants to borrow something, Jared has an issue. "Come on, you loan stuff to your friends all the time," his brother whines. It isn't that Jared thinks his brother won't take care of it or return it – it's just that he is such a pain sometimes and it's hard for him to do something nice for him. Hmm, he could loan him the hockey stick and ask for something in return – for example make his brother do his chores. But, the right thing to do – the Jesus thing to do – is to loan him the stick with no strings attached.

FEAR OR TRUST?

> "You of little faith, why are you so afraid?"
> Matthew 8:26

You'd think that Jesus' disciples would have a really strong faith. After all, they were with Him when He healed people and when He raised dead people back to life. They were there when He fed the 5,000 with 5 fish and 2 loaves of bread. They knew that He could do pretty much anything!

However, they were humans and sometimes they got scared that Jesus wasn't going to take care of them. It must have made Him sad that their faith wasn't stronger since they knew so much about Him.

LIVING IT

Think about this. The disciples lived with Jesus for 3½ years and saw everything that He did and they heard everything He taught. Yet, their faith wasn't able to keep them from being afraid sometimes. You have the entire Bible to read that tells everything He did in those 3½ years and more. Is your faith stronger than theirs? You may still get scared sometimes. You may wonder where He is sometimes. That's OK, just go back to the Bible and read about His strength, power and love for you. Then, ask Him to help you trust Him more and more.

September 26

> "Take heart, daughter," He said, "your faith has healed you."
> Matthew 9:22

When problems and crises come many people start praying. Even people who have never prayed before start praying.

They ask God to solve their problems and fix their situations. They may be surprised when He doesn't answer their prayers. But, here is the key – faith.

Spouting a prayer when life gets tough but having no relationship with Jesus before or after that prayer, is not faith in action. It is desperation. Faith is what healed the woman Jesus was speaking to here – not desperation.

LIVING IT

Jacob's parents are getting a divorce. Jacob is desperate to stop it. He loves both of his parents and doesn't want their family to split up. Jacob has never prayed before, but he begins begging God to fix the problem. "Make them love each other again." But, it doesn't happen and the divorce goes through. Does this mean God doesn't care? No. He cares a lot. But what He cares about most is having a relationship with Jacob – not one where he shoots up prayers of desperation, but one where he talks with God often, reads His Word and learns to trust Him and find comfort and peace in Him.

September 27

AS YOU GO ...

> "As you go, preach this message: 'The kingdom of heaven is near.'"
> Matthew 10:7

Jesus often spoke about the work He has for His followers. That work is to tell others about the love of God and help them find a way to know and follow Him.

The cool thing about this statement is that Jesus just assumes His followers will be obediently going to do the work. He says, "As you go" so He expects you to be obedient in telling others.

LIVING IT

Adam doesn't have a clue about how to tell others about Jesus. And, he isn't exactly sure what "the kingdom of heaven is near" actually means. So, he asks his pastor for advice. Pastor said, "Adam, let your friends know that you do love Jesus. Let them know that He is a part of your everyday life and is important to you. Live your life so they can see His values. As far as the kingdom of heaven being near – it is. It's close to you, because Jesus lives in your heart and one day soon He will come back to earth to get His family and take us to heaven with Him."

September 28

> "It will not be you speaking, but the Spirit of your Father speaking through you."
>
> Matthew 10:20

There will be times when people attack your faith and you simply do not know how to defend yourself or God.

Jesus said to stay super close to God and rely on the Holy Spirit in those times. He will give you the right words to speak. He will help you be courageous but respectful, strong but kind and His words will actually be the words of God, spoken through your lips!

LIVING IT

Rusty dreads science class because his teacher doesn't believe in God or the Bible. He is absolutely sure that evolution is true and that God had nothing to do with the creation of anything. He gets pretty sarcastic to any student who challenges him or even mentions God. Rusty wants to state his faith in God, but he is scared. He doesn't know what to say. So, Rusty follows Jesus' advice and asks God to give him the right words and the right time to speak up. Guess what? **He does!** Rusty respectfully, but strongly states his faith in Jesus and the truth of the Bible!

September 29

FENCE RIDERS

> "Whoever disowns Me before men, I will disown him before My Father in heaven."
>
> Matthew 10:33

This is serious business. Jesus warns people not to take their relationship with Him lightly. If you think you can kind of stay on the fence; not committing or denying your belief in Jesus, you can be sure the day will come when you'll have to take a stand.

If you deny Jesus because you're too embarrassed or scared to say what you believe, then don't expect Him to stick up for you, either.

Get in or get out – there is no riding the fence here.

LIVING IT

Todd thinks he can keep everyone happy. When he is with his Christian friends, he talks about God, prays for his meals and promises to pray for friends' problems. He knows all the lingo and the right actions. But, when he is with his non-Christian friends it all goes out the window. He speaks and behaves just like they do and brags that he wants nothing to do with God! Todd tries to have it both ways. Guess what? That doesn't work. Take a stand for Jesus, Todd!

September 30

OCTOBER

> "Go back and report to John what you hear and see: The blind receive sight, the lame walk, those who have leprosy are cured, the deaf hear, the dead are raised, and the good news is preached to the poor."
>
> Matthew 11:4-5

Jesus instructed His followers to bear witness to His work. What does that mean?

Just as a witness in a court case testifies of what he has seen or heard, a witness of Jesus', work testifies of His work so that others may believe in His strength and power. Then they may believe that He is God's Son and that He came to earth to show love for mankind and make a way for people to know God.

LIVING IT

"You sound so sure that Jesus is real. How do you know for sure?" Darius asked Jake. "Seriously, the Bible could just be a bunch of stories. How do you know it's true?"

Jake had an answer. He could testify of Jesus' work in his life and God's answers to his prayers. He could tell Darius how God had directed and guided him. So, Jake bears witness to Jesus' work so that Darius will know He is real!

SMOOTH TALKERS

"You brood of vipers, how can you who are evil say anything good? For out of the overflow of the heart the mouth speaks."
Matthew 12:34

Jesus is speaking to smooth talkers. You know the type. They know exactly the right things to say all the time, but Jesus knows there is no sincerity in what they say.

They may say things that make them appear to honor and love God, but their hearts are far away from Him. Eventually the wickedness and evil in their hearts comes out in their words or actions.

Remember, Jesus sees your heart and while you can fool people, you can never fool God.

LIVING IT

Cade is a smooth talker. He knows how to say all the right things, no matter who he is with. With adults he says humble and respectful things, but even by the tone of his voice people know he doesn't mean it.

With other guys he tries to sound like he is their buddy and cares about them. They don't buy it either. He even tries to fool God with his smooth talk. But God looks at his heart and knows that Cade is just a smooth talker whose heart does not belong to Jesus.

October 2

> "Whoever does the will of my Father in heaven is My brother and sister and mother."
> Matthew 12:50

People who obey God and serve Him are His family members.

Jesus was not dismissing His earthly family – after all, He asked a friend to take care of His mother before He died – but He was emphasizing how close He is to His obedient followers.

They become part of His family. How cool is that? Obeying God makes you a family member!

LIVING IT

Do you think obeying all the things Jesus teaches in the Bible is a really big job? Yeah it is. But if you want to be in His family, you have to be serious about living for Him.

How? Begin with one thing – like honoring your mom and dad as Jesus teaches you to do. Then work on loving others more than yourself. Be honest and fair with others. Be compassionate and caring. Doing God's will can begin by learning one thing at a time.

October 3

SECRETS!

> "The knowledge of the secrets of the kingdom of heaven has been given to you, but not to them."
>
> Matthew 13:11

Jesus was speaking to normal, every-day people when He said this. He was not speaking to the religious leaders who criticized His every move.

Isn't it cool that the secrets of heaven are given to normal people who have seeking hearts? People who want to know Him better?

The religious leaders who thought they had all the answers would not understand the messages of Jesus' stories because their hearts didn't want to know God better. They just wanted to be in control, even of Jesus. That didn't happen.

LIVING IT

I'm just a kid, Jeremy thought, *so how can I understand the lessons of the Bible? I love Jesus and I want to obey Him, but I'm just a kid.*

Jeremy is much closer than he thinks! Having a heart that wants to know God puts him miles ahead of someone who thinks he has all the answers already. Jeremy's seeking heart is the heart to which God will reveal the deeper meanings of Scripture.

October 4

A CALLOUSED HEART

"For this people's heart has become calloused; they hardly hear with their ears, and they have closed their eyes. Otherwise they might see with their eyes, hear with their ears, understand with their hearts and turn, and I would heal them."

Matthew 13:15

A calloused heart is one that has grown a thick, hard-to-penetrate shell around it. It cares only for itself and can't be touched by the truth of God's Word or care for other people.

It's a sad condition which will keep the person apart from God. It isn't hopeless though.

If this person could open his heart to Jesus, He would heal that calloused heart and be able to see and hear the truth of Jesus' love.

LIVING IT

Jordy has been gently telling his friend, Jimmy about Jesus. Jimmy has heard the message of Jesus' love. He has talked with Jordy about his faith, but he says it just doesn't make any sense to him. Jordy thinks Jimmy's heart might be calloused, just like this verse says.

Jimmy hasn't had an easy life and he might be blaming God for that. So, now Jordy prays for Jesus' love to break through that thick skin on Jimmy's heart so that he can understand how very much Jesus loves him!

COMPLETE SURRENDER

> "Whoever wants to save his life will lose it, but whoever loses his life for Me will find it."
> Matthew 16:25

You can't follow Jesus and hold some part of yourself back from Him.

Complete surrender means giving up your wants, hopes, dreams, time, activities and passions to Jesus. Then trying to learn what He wants you to do, how He wants you to live, how He wants you to treat others and learn to love Him.

So, while it may seem as though you are giving up your life, or at least control of your life, you are actually gaining the joy of living for Jesus and the promise of eternal life with Him!

LIVING IT

When Andy asked Jesus to be his Savior, he meant it and really intended to follow Him. But, there was one part of his life that he just couldn't give up control of – his friendships. A couple of guys who were important friends to Andy sometimes pulled him into activities that were disrespectful to other guys and definitely not honoring to God.

Until Andy can give God that part of his life, too, and pull away from those friends, he will not be completely surrendered to God and will not find his new life.

October 6

THE FAITH OF A CHILD

> "I tell you the truth, unless you change and become like little children, you will never enter the kingdom of heaven."
>
> Matthew 18:3

Powerful, important, strong people who are only concerned about themselves do not impress Jesus.

People who think they have all the answers are not dependent on Jesus. They don't think they need Him.

Children who are dependent and trusting and who desire to honor Jesus by obeying Him are the ones who please Him. Jesus points out that these little children have a place in heaven.

LIVING IT

Corey does not have all the answers to life. In fact, he has more questions than he has answers. Corey accepted Jesus as Savior. He quickly began to feel like Jesus was his best friend. He began to want to spend time with Jesus and get to know Him better and better.

Corey knows that Jesus has the answers to life. He knows he needs to learn from Jesus and he can't wait to do that!

October 7

ROLE-MODEL RESPONSIBILITIES

> "Woe to the world because of the things that cause people to sin! Such things must come, but woe to the man through whom they come!"
>
> Matthew 18:7

Jesus knew that some people have enough influence to cause others to sin. That's true even of kids. You have influence over others, especially someone who is younger and looks up to you.

So, if you encourage another guy to do something wrong either by encouraging him to do it or by giving him an example of doing wrong, you will answer to Jesus for it.

LIVING IT

Tony is a couple of years younger than Ben and looks up to him a lot. He does everything that Ben does. He tries to dress like Ben and talk like Ben. When Tony heard Ben using some language that wasn't very nice, he started saying the same things. Tony thought he was being cool like Ben. He was wrong. He was actually being mean to other people and disrespectful to God. Both Ben and Tony will have to answer to Jesus for their words, but Ben will answer more for leading Tony down that path.

October 8

> "In the same way your Father in heaven is not willing that any of these little ones should be lost."
> Matthew 18:14

Jesus was explaining to His disciples how much God loves all people.

He pulled a small child into the room. He then explained that just as a shepherd would leave 99 sheep on a hillside to go find one sheep that had wandered away, there is a party in heaven each time one person accepts Jesus.

This Scripture verse was the closing of that example. God wants every single person, adult and child to know Him.

LIVING IT

Brody did not feel special at all. He was the middle child in a family of six children so he often got lost in the crowd. Brody wasn't extra good at anything. He was an average student, average singer, average athlete and average conversationalist. He was average.

But, when Brody started to understand that God wanted him (him!) to know Him, he felt anything but average! The truth is that God didn't want Brody to be lost. He wanted him in heaven. For the first time in his life, Brody felt special!

October 9

PRAYER PARTNERS

"I tell you that if two of you on earth agree about anything you ask for, it will be done for you by My Father in heaven."

Matthew 18:19

Is Jesus saying that there is power in numbers? Not necessarily. Is He saying that if you get a friend to join you He will give you anything you want? Nope. Well, then what is He saying?

He is emphasizing how good it is to share your prayer requests with others. There is a comfort in knowing that someone else is praying with you about something important – and even to actually pray together.

It's good to be a part of a community of believers.

LIVING IT

Eric feels like a loser and he is very lonely. His family doesn't pay much attention to him. He doesn't have many friends, but it doesn't take many. One friend notices that Eric is not doing well. So, one afternoon while they were shooting hoops this friend asked Eric what was going on. Eric hesitantly told his friend why he felt like a loser. His friend said, "Well, you're not a loser. And, you do have a friend – me! I'll pray with you for more friends and more successes in your life. We'll beat this together!"

> "Where two or three come together in My name, there am I with them."
>
> Matthew 18:20

You've seen it over and over – Jesus is all about relationships.

The Christian life is not intended to be lived by yourself, separated from others. Jesus encourages people of similar beliefs and passions to join together in prayer, worship and service to Him.

One person can accomplish some things, but a group of people can encourage one another and help one another to accomplish so much more!

LIVING IT

CJ's attention has been grabbed by news stories of the children in the homeless shelters in his city. For some reason, they just grab his heart and he wants to do something for them. But, what? There are so many of them and he is just one person.

Then, CJ has an idea. He gets several of his friends and their parents to join with him. They hold car washes and work days to hire themselves out to work for people. All the money they earn is used to buy winter coats, mittens and hats, and one small toy to be delivered to the shelters for the children. CJ is happy that his friends have helped.

TO INFINITY AND BEYOND!

> "I tell you, not seven times, but seventy-seven times."
>
> Matthew 18:22

Peter had just asked Jesus how many times he had to forgive someone who had wronged him.

Peter thought seven times of forgiveness was good. Jesus disagreed with him. Seventy-seven times seems like a lot of forgiveness, doesn't it? That's the point.

Forgive and forgive and forgive, because that's what Jesus does for you. Forgive over and over to the point that you lose count, because keeping score is not the point. Forgiveness and restoring the relationship is the point.

LIVING IT

"I'm so done with Doug!" Julio shouted. "He thinks he's so funny. He's always putting me down and then says he's just teasing. I'm tired of it!" Mom listened quietly then said, "Maybe he doesn't know he is hurting your feelings. Why don't you talk with him? You've been friends a long time." "Yeah," Julio interrupted, "and I've forgiven him like a billion times. No more!" "Julio, forgiveness doesn't have a limit. Doug is your friend. Talk with him and give him another chance. Just like God does for you," Mom said.

> "The servant's master took pity on him, canceled the debt and let him go."
> Matthew 18:27

Jesus gave an example of true forgiveness by telling the story of a man who owed money to a king, but was unable to pay it back.

The man fell on his knees and begged the king's forgiveness. He asked for the king's patience and promised to pay back every cent. The king had mercy on him and canceled the debt completely and let him go! True forgiveness forgets as well as forgives. The debt is completely gone.

LIVING IT

"Aaron, I forgive you for what you did," Rex said. "But, I didn't ask your forgiveness," Aaron said, "and I don't deserve it. What I did was mean and sneaky. Why are you forgiving me? Why aren't you trying to get even with me?"

Rex just smiled because he knew he was doing the Jesus thing. "Nope, I want to forgive you. Let's just get on with our friendship," he said.

October 13

FORGIVE LIKE JESUS

> "Shouldn't you have had mercy on your fellow servant just as I had on you?"
> Matthew 18:33

Jesus told this story of a king who forgave a huge debt that a servant owed him. Then the servant turned around and had another man thrown in jail for a small debt owed to him. Where is the justice in that?

Since the man received grace for a big debt, why didn't he offer the other man grace for a small debt? The bottom line is to forgive others because you have been forgiven.

LIVING IT

Hayden broke his mother's favorite lamp. He felt terrible because it had belonged to Grandma and Hayden knew it was very special to his mom. Hayden apologized to his mom and asked her forgiveness. Mom was very sad, but she forgave Hayden.

Later that night Hayden's brother accidently broke a toy trophy in Hayden's room. Hayden went crazy and yelled at him. Mom stepped in and reminded Hayden that she had forgiven him for something big, so perhaps Hayden should forgive his brother for this small thing.

SINCERE FORGIVENESS

> "This is how My heavenly Father will treat each of you unless you forgive your brother from your heart."
>
> Matthew 18:35

This is how Jesus ended His story about the man who was forgiven for his large debt and then refused to forgive someone who owed him a little bit of money.

Jesus said that God notices that kind of selfishness and it is pretty useless to ask God to forgive you if you refuse to truly and honestly forgive others.

In Jesus' story, the unforgiving man is tortured and thrown into jail. Not a pretty picture, is it?

LIVING IT

Alan was really mad at Len. So angry that he wanted to hurt him. He wanted to make all their friends mad at Len, too. But, just as he was ready to tell everyone what Len had done, Len asked Alan to forgive him. He said he was sorry for what he had done. So, Alan said, "OK, I forgive you." But he didn't mean it. Alan still had a lot of anger in his heart and he still tried to get their friends on his side by bad-mouthing Len. How did that turn out for him? His friends got mad at him for not being honest and for not forgiving Len when he asked. They all dumped Alan. Forgiveness must be sincere or it isn't forgiveness at all.

October 15

WHAT IS GOOD?

"Why do you ask Me about what is good?" Jesus replied. "There is only One who is good. If you want to enter life, obey the commandments."

Matthew 19:17

God is in a category all by Himself. What respect, honor and worship He commands!

Jesus said this to a rich man who asked Him how to get eternal life. Jesus quickly pointed out that it's important to recognize God's goodness and give Him the honor He deserves.

Because of that honor, you obey the commandments God has given and then respect, honor and obedience leads you to eternal life.

LIVING IT

"Yeah, I want to have eternal life. I'm just a kid now, but I'd like to know that someday I'm going to heaven," Scottie says. But, is Scottie willing to commit to recognizing God as the only One who is truly good? The only One who is perfect and sinless and loving and kind and honest and fair?

Is Scottie willing to learn God's commandments which are given in the Bible and then to obey them? Those are necessary steps to receiving eternal life and living for Jesus. Scottie needs to make the choice to honor and obey God.

October 16

> "Do not murder, do not commit adultery, do not steal, do not give false testimony, honor your father and mother, and 'love your neighbor as yourself.'"
> Matthew 19:18-19

Jesus reviews six of the Ten Commandments here – the six that involve how you treat others.

He reviews them for the rich man who asked what commandments he needed to obey to get eternal life. It's interesting that Jesus mentioned the commandments about relating to other people rather than the ones that focus on how to relate to God.

He knew that face-to-face relationships could be even harder to maintain than a spiritual relationship with Christ. However, it's important to have healthy relationships with others.

LIVING IT

I'm good, thought Peter. *I haven't murdered anyone or committed adultery or stolen anything.* Yep, Peter thought he was doing OK. However, he conveniently skipped over the command to honor his father and mother. His disrespect and unkind words to them last night didn't cross his mind. He was angry because they made him do his homework and chores before he could play video games. And the last command, to love his neighbor as himself, well, that one he wasn't always so good at either. Peter needs to pay attention to the whole list – not just the easy ones.

SELLING YOUR STUFF

"If you want to be perfect, go, sell your possessions and give to the poor, and you will have treasure in heaven. Then come, follow Me."

Matthew 19:21

This is Jesus' final answer to the rich man who wanted to know how to get eternal life.

Jesus focused the man's attention on caring for others. People can divide their hearts so that with one part they praise God, speak about loving Him and obeying Him. But with the other part they disregard other people, holding on to their possessions, showing that they do not care for others at all.

Caring for others is important. Jesus makes that clear.

LIVING IT

Rick understood what Jesus meant by giving to the poor. Rick and his buddies organized a garage sale in their church. They gathered stuff from the whole church. But Rick even encouraged his buddies to sell some of their own things that were pretty nice – things that maybe they liked. He said, "All of us have so much stuff and there are some kids who don't even have warm clothes, let alone toys. Let's sell our stuff to raise money to buy things other kids need." Rick's friends joined in and they sold enough to raise $500 to give to a mission that helped kids.

> "I tell you the truth, it is hard for a rich man to enter the kingdom of heaven."
>
> Matthew 19:23

Why would Jesus say this? Aren't rich people important and powerful? Don't they get whatever they want?

Sure, wealthy people are often important and powerful. Wealthy people often feel that they can get whatever they want. They may be able to buy what they want or have people scurry to please them and give them things or do things for them.

So, rich people may not see the need to depend on God or trust Him for their needs. That's why it would be hard for a rich person to enter heaven.

LIVING IT

Maybe you're thinking that there is nothing wrong with getting what you want. Jesus' point is that an important part of being in God's family, is the need to trust Him. Completely. The reason it's hard for people with a lot of money to trust God is that they are accustomed to getting what they want, because they can buy what they want. They expect others to listen to them because their money gives them power. But God doesn't do what anyone tells Him to do. Coming to faith in Jesus takes a certain level of humility and sometimes that is hard for wealthy people.

October 19

FIRST IS LAST

Powerful, important, famous, influential, wealthy. These are all words that describe people who are used to being first. They are used to being respected, honored and getting their way.

The people who are usually last are not as wealthy. They are quieter, humble, sacrificing, concerned for others, not as powerful, not famous, average people. People in this group more easily trust God and give to others.

This group, because of their dependence on and trust in God and concern for others, will be first in God's kingdom.

LIVING IT

Martin wants to be important. He pushes guys he considers unimportant out of his way. He pays no attention to anyone who can't do something for him. He thinks he's first and best, but he's really last from Jesus' perspective. Derrick on the other hand, cares a lot for other people. He notices kids who are off by themselves and tries to draw them in to games or even conversation. He gives his time to help others wherever he can. Derrick is on the road to being first, but that doesn't really matter to him. It isn't why he does what he does.

October 20

> "I tell you the truth, if you have faith and do not doubt, not only can you do what was done to the fig tree, but also you can say to this mountain, 'Go, throw yourself into the sea,' and it will be done."
>
> Matthew 21:21

Jesus had just declared that a fig tree would never grow fruit again and He told His followers that if they just had enough faith they could do the same thing or even make a mountain fall into the sea.

The incredible power of Jesus is available to His followers. You can move mountains if you just have enough faith.

But, how does a guy learn to have faith that big? Practice. Trust. Depend. Believe.

LIVING IT

Brad loves God and he would love to be able to make a difference in the world for God. "If I had power like Jesus, I would use it to help people with problems and to help others come to know Him," he says. Brad would do that, too. He wants to learn to have bigger and bigger faith.

So, he starts small by trusting God with small things like helping him get over having nightmares. Every time Brad sees God answer a prayer, protect him or help him, his faith grows a little bigger. It's a journey to learn and grow in faith and Brad is on the right track.

BE CAREFUL HOW YOU LIVE

Watch out for teachers who do not practice what they preach. Jesus warns you to make sure that the teachers you listen to live in ways that match what they teach.

Some people like to tell others what to do, but they won't do a single thing to help make sure the work gets done. These types of people have way too much pride.

"You must obey them and do everything they tell you. But do not do what they do, for they do not practice what they preach. They tie up heavy loads and put them on men's shoulders, but they themselves are not willing to lift a finger to move them."

Matthew 23:3-4

LIVING IT

It is a big responsibility to be a teacher who tries to help people understand how to know God and live for Him. Teachers who tell others how to live for God, but those whose own lives don't match those guidelines will answer to God for their hypocrisy.

A teacher worth listening to is willing to work hard, get dirty and tired to get the work done – just as he expects his workers to do. Be careful what teachers you follow and be careful how you live. Don't say one thing is right, but live in a way that shows you don't really believe it.

October 22

> "Everything they do is done for men to see."
> Matthew 23:5

Jesus is talking about religious leaders who make a big show of being religious. They show off religious things, but only when they are sure that others are watching. They want other people to notice how religious they are and think they are super important. They want places of honor so that people will treat them as though they are really important. Everything they do is for their own sake, not for God at all.

LIVING IT

Rob is pretty impressed with himself. He wants everyone around him to think he is important and influential. Sometimes he does things that make it "look" like he really cares about others, but he really doesn't.

Everything Rob does is for show – to make himself look important and powerful. He doesn't do stuff for God or for others. Rob will definitely answer to God for this behavior. It's contrary to everything Jesus teaches.

October 23

ONE FATHER

> "Do not call anyone on earth 'father,' for you have one Father, and He is in heaven."
>
> Matthew 23:9

God is the supreme authority in the world and He won't share that position with anyone or anything else.

God expects respect and worship and love that is greater than what is given to any earthly person. Of course, this statement does not mean that you do not respect your father. It simply means that you should never put a human on an equal level with God.

LIVING IT

Hopefully you have a good relationship with your dad. You may think he can do anything and that he is the smartest guy in the whole world. That's good. You should respect him and learn from him. In fact, a good relationship with your dad can help you understand your relationship with your heavenly Father.

But, your dad should never be more important to you than your heavenly Father. Keep God in first place.

October 24

> "Watch out that no one deceives you."
> Matthew 24:4

Sadly, there are people who actually try to get people to follow them instead of Jesus. They create their own religions (often called cults), but they pretend to be teaching people about Jesus.

Jesus warns His followers to be careful of the teachers they listen to by testing what they teach against the Bible and making sure their teachings agree with the Bible.

If you ever have questions about a teacher, ask God to guide you and also talk to someone you respect for advice.

LIVING IT

Perry's brother has always been a strong Christian, but since he went away to college he has gotten kind of weird. He got involved with a group at his school that just seems kind of off-center from what Perry and his parents believe. His brother doesn't even talk with his parents very often. He won't ever talk about this group and what they believe.

Perry is afraid that his brother has been taken in by a false teacher. He prays for wisdom and for his brother's eyes to be opened.

BE READY

"No one knows about that day or hour, not even the angels in heaven, nor the Son, but only the Father."

Matthew 24:36

Jesus is God's Son, but there are some things God has not even told Jesus – for example, the time when Jesus will come back to earth to take His followers to heaven.

If Jesus doesn't know – and He says that only God knows – then it makes sense that no human knows when that day will come. People who claim to be able to predict the day when Jesus will return are mistaken and should not be listened to.

LIVING IT

Jamie knows that Jesus will come back one day to take His followers to heaven. He's read that in the Bible. Jamie has heard of people who say that they know when that will happen. So far they've all been wrong. But, some people listen to them anyway and sell all their stuff and just wait for Jesus to come. It's weird. Jamie knows that he should just be ready to go with Jesus whenever He does come. Jamie reads his Bible and tries his best to obey its teachings. He prays and stays close to Jesus. Jamie can't wait to see Jesus face to face!

October 26

FUTURE REWARDS

"Then the King will say to those on his right, 'Come, you who are blessed by My Father; take your inheritance, the kingdom prepared for you since the creation of the world.'"
Matthew 25:34

This is a wonderful promise from Jesus. He will come back to earth one day to get His followers and take them to heaven. Jesus promises that His followers will receive the rewards and blessings of eternal life with Him.

God has been preparing the kingdom of heaven for Jesus' followers since the beginning of time. It is a beautiful place to spend forever with Jesus!

LIVING IT

Following Jesus is not always easy. You may have problems just because you have chosen to accept Jesus. People may give you a hard time about that choice. Jesus will walk with you every step of the way and teach you how to follow Him.

One step at a time is enough for your faith to grow deeper. Jesus promises that not only will He be with you every day of your life, He is preparing a special place for you to be with Him in heaven forever!

October 27

SHARING JESUS' LOVE

Jesus always emphasized the necessity of His followers caring for others. An important part of living for Jesus is taking care of others and especially people who are poor and lonely.

People who are undesirable and need a lot of help are the ones Jesus wants you to reach out to, not just your friends or people who are in pretty good shape anyway. By helping these people, you show your love for Jesus.

"I was hungry and you gave Me something to eat, I was thirsty and you gave Me something to drink, I was a stranger and you invited Me in, I needed clothes and you clothed Me, I was sick and you looked after Me, I was in prison and you came to visit Me."

Matthew 25:35-36

LIVING IT

Donating to a food pantry, serving meals to homeless people, collecting clothing for those who need it, visiting sick people and running errands for them, visiting prisoners or the families of prisoners, giving to ministries that take care of poor or sick people around the world.

There are so many ways to help others and share Jesus' love with others. Just look around and see how you can get involved.

October 28

"The King will reply, 'I tell you the truth, whatever you did for one of the least of these brothers of Mine, you did for Me.'"
Matthew 25:40

Jesus had just listed several wonderful things that people had done – feeding the hungry, clothing the naked, caring for the sick and visiting those in prison.

Now He says that when they did those kind things for other people they were really serving Him. That's amazing!

Jesus emphasizes over and over how important it is to care for others and now He says that caring for others actually shows your love for Him!

LIVING IT

Does it seem amazing that helping other people can be the same as helping Jesus? Remember that several times Jesus said it's easy to be kind to your friends. Anyone can do that.

But, when you step out of your comfort zone and help people who you don't know or people who may be a bit less desirable because they are dirty, stinky or sick – well, then more than ever you are showing your love for Jesus.

A FRESH START

"No one sews a patch of unshrunk cloth on an old garment. If he does, the new piece will pull away from the old, making the tear worse."

Mark 2:21

The teachings of Jesus were different from what people had heard before. His teachings were pretty much the opposite of what the religious leaders taught.

So, Jesus said that it wouldn't work to take His new teachings of humility and love and just try to wrap them into your current way of life. Following Jesus meant starting fresh with Him.

LIVING IT

Norm wants to follow Jesus, well, kind of. What he is trying to do is keep living his life the way he always has – with all his old attitudes, old habits and old friends, but just add Jesus in. Yeah, it doesn't work that way.

Norm soon finds that trying to add Jesus in to the way his life is now just causes problems with him and his friends. Norm needs to let Jesus take over his whole life so he can have a fresh start with Jesus at the center of his life. Then everything will change for the better.

"With the measure you use, it will be measured to you – and even more."

Mark 4:24

What kind of measuring stick do you use to judge other people? Is it a pretty short stick that does not give them much room to make mistakes or to disappoint you? Did you know that the way you judge other people is the same way you will be judged? Does that make you want to be a little more forgiving and understanding of others? Good.

LIVING IT

What does "measuring stick" mean? It is describing the standards you judge other people by. For example, do you judge someone by how cool he is, how intelligent, how kind, how loyal of a friend? Do you judge people for being too critical, too selfish, too self-centered?

Yeah, those are the same things you will be judged for. Don't expect God to cut you slack if you're critical and judgmental of others.

October 31

> "Why are you so afraid? Do you still have no faith?"
> Mark 4:40

Jesus asked His disciples this after He had calmed a storm on the sea. He had just done an amazing miracle – seriously – the weather did what He told it to do!

They had seen Him do other miracles before this. His disciples had traveled with Him and heard all His teachings, but they still didn't trust Him enough to keep them from being afraid.

He must have wondered what else He had to do or say to get them to trust Him completely.

LIVING IT

OK, same kind of story. Kyle prayed for help in making new friends. That prayer was answered. Then he prayed for help in making the soccer team. He made it. He prayed for his dad to find a new job. He did. He prayed for his grandpa to get well. He did.

Yeah, you'd think that Kyle's faith would get stronger and stronger, but he still got scared every time a new challenge came. He should have known he could trust God, and he's getting there. It's a process.

November 1

MY WAY

"You have a fine way of setting aside the commands of God in order to observe your own traditions!"
Mark 7:9

Jesus has a way with words, doesn't He? He almost seems to be giving a compliment (but He isn't) to people who make up their own rules about how to live the Christian life.

They might twist God's commands just a bit to fit their own rules or they may totally toss God's commands in the garbage. Either way it's wrong. They are not truly obeying God and they will answer to Him for their selfishness.

LIVING IT

"It's no big deal to say things about other people if it makes my friends laugh. Laughter is good for the soul!" Mark declared. He was trying to justify his unkind words about some kids in his class.

Mark is wrong. He should know what God says about watching his speech and loving others. Unkind words – even if they are funny – are not loving. That means they are not obedient to God's teachings.

November 2

DIRTY ON THE INSIDE

"From within, out of men's hearts, come evil thoughts, sexual immorality, theft, murder, adultery, greed, malice, deceit, lewdness, envy, slander, arrogance and folly. All these evils come from inside and make a man 'unclean.'"

Mark 7:21-23

Sin starts on the inside, because the truth is, you make a choice in your heart to disobey before you ever act on it. It's your choice.

You can walk away from a tempting situation, or you can stick around and let the temptation take hold in your heart. Once that happens you're going to do it and that is what makes you unclean in God's sight.

LIVING IT

Tanner knows the difference between right and wrong. His parents have taught him that all his life. But, when he started hanging around with some guys who didn't care about Jesus, some of their bad habits began rubbing off on him even though he tried to keep them out of his life.

One of those bad habits was how he used God's name – as a joke or even as a swear word. Tanner knew better, but he wanted to fit in with his friends so he chose to speak like them. Misusing God's name is sin. Tanner chose it. He did it.

PRACTICAL COMPASSION

> "I have compassion for these people; they have already been with Me three days and have nothing to eat."
>
> Mark 8:2

Jesus is so practical. He knew that the thousands of people around Him that day had come to hear Him teach and to see Him do miracles.

But, He also knew that they needed food. They couldn't really listen to what He was teaching if they were hungry.

Jesus wanted their physical needs met as well as their spiritual needs. Pretty cool, huh? If He did that for them, He will do it for you.

LIVING IT

Jesus may want you to be part of the solution to meet the physical needs of others. If your needs are all met – you have a home, clothes and food – then look around your town, county, state, world. You will find people who don't have their needs met. How can you help? Collect food for a food pantry? Give money to organizations that supply food? Pack boxes of food that go overseas? Organize a group to do all those things? Whatever Jesus plants in your heart, He will help you do because He cares about physical needs as well as spiritual needs.

November 4

> "Who do people say I am? But, what about you? Who do you say I am?"
> Mark 8:27, 29

Jesus asked Peter, one of His closest followers what the word on the street was about Him.

He had done all kinds of miracles in God's name. He had taught about God and how to live for Him. So He wondered if people were getting it. Had they begun to believe that He is God's Son, the Messiah, who came to save the world?

A couple of verses later Jesus asked Peter, "OK, who do you say I am?" Peter was one of Jesus' closest friends – did he get it?

LIVING IT

Richard knows who Jesus is. At least he thinks he does. His parents are Christians and have taught him that Jesus is the Son of God who died for his sins and rose back to life. They taught that He is Richard's Savior and that He will come one day to take all His children to heaven.

Yes, that's what they taught Richard. But, he doesn't read his Bible, doesn't pray, doesn't think about Jesus at all most of the time. So, while his head may know who Jesus is, his heart says He is no one special. What does your heart say? Who is Jesus to you?

FOLLOW JESUS

> "If anyone would come after Me, he must deny himself and take up his cross and follow Me."
> Mark 8:34

What was Jesus talking about? What does it mean to deny yourself?

The Christian life is one of surrender. Denying yourself means surrendering your will and desires to whatever Christ wants for your life.

Taking up your cross means being willing to serve Christ in the way He leads you even when life gets tough. Even when you don't want to do stuff. Even when you're tired. Follow Jesus. You'll never regret it.

LIVING IT

Aaron didn't get what Jesus was talking about until he got recruited for a traveling soccer team. He was pretty excited about it and even felt honored to be recruited. But, this team practiced every Sunday morning. That meant no church.

Should Aaron say yes to the team and just let church go? Or, should he choose church? His parents left it up to him, even though he knew what they wanted him to do. Denying his own wants and taking up his cross for Aaron in this situation meant saying no to the soccer team.

November 6

> "Whoever wants to save his life will lose it, but whoever loses his life for Me and for the gospel will save it."
>
> Mark 8:35

Some people feel that to give up control over their own lives means they are losing their lives. Because they have given up control it may feel as though they are free falling in space. It's scary.

But, when you give up control to Jesus then you are really saving your life. You are turning from sin and from the hopelessness of a life without Him in it that has no hope of heaven. Giving your life to Jesus actually gives you purpose and direction. It saves your life rather than losing it.

LIVING IT

Duane has control issues. He knows it, too. He likes to be in charge by telling his friends what they should do, how they should think and what they should say. His room has everything in its place and he pretty much knows what his plan is for every day, week and month.

So, giving up control of his life to Jesus did not happen easily. He fought it in fact. He even tried to tell Jesus what to do. Yeah, that didn't work so well. Once Duane was able to surrender control though, he found his life had more purpose in it every day. He didn't lose his life. He found it!

CARING FOR ALL

> "Whoever welcomes one of these little children in My name welcomes Me; and whoever welcomes Me does not welcome Me but the One who sent Me."
>
> Mark 9:37

During Jesus' time on earth children, women, sick people and poor people were considered unimportant by powerful people and even by religious leaders.

Healthy, wealthy men were the important ones. But not to Jesus. When He saw some children nearby He took the opportunity to point out that people who cared about them were actually caring about Him and His Father.

Jesus cared about those who were unimportant to others and He wanted His followers to do the same.

LIVING IT

It must be hard to be the new guy in school, thought Adam. He had noticed a new boy in his class who was always alone. *He must be pretty lonely*. He wondered what it would be like to be new in a school and have no friends at all.

None of the other guys wanted to talk to the new boy. But, Adam remembered that Jesus said to care about all people, so he asked the new boy to sit by him at lunchtime and they talked some. It felt good to be nice to someone who was ignored by others.

> "I tell you the truth, anyone who will not receive the kingdom of God like a little child will never enter it."
>
> Mark 10:15

Maybe you've heard the old saying, "he toots his own horn." It means that a guy who is full of pride in himself makes sure everyone knows how important and special he is.

Jesus isn't impressed with a person who is impressed with himself. To be great in God's kingdom one must be humble and filled with trust in Him.

LIVING IT

If you asked Dan if he has a problem with pride, he would say, "No." But when his friends think about it they realize that Dan talks about himself all the time. He always has to be the center of attention. He usually has a story that is better than what anyone else tells. Dan is not humble and he doesn't trust God completely, because he feels that he can pretty much handle anything that happens by himself. After all, he is Dan the Man!

Yeah, Dan will soon learn that humility, faith, trust and love are more important than always being Number One.

THE COMMANDMENTS

"You know the commandments: 'Do not murder, do not commit adultery, do not steal, do not give false testimony, do not defraud, honor your father and mother.'"

Mark 10:19

A rich man asked Jesus how to know if he would have eternal life.

Jesus first focused the man's thoughts on how he treated others. Was he kind, was he fair, was he moral? Did he treat others with the respect and honor they deserved?

It matters to Jesus how people treat one another. Love for God is shown not just by how you treat Him, but also by how you treat others.

LIVING IT

Lance is pretty good at keeping the commandments, at least the ones Jesus mentioned here except maybe for the one on false testimony. Does he sometimes bend the truth a little? Yep. Does he join in conversation that would be considered gossip about other guys? Yep. Does he even stretch the truth when talking about someone else just to make his story good or make himself look better? Yep.

Maybe Lance needs to reconsider how well he is obeying the commandments. Maybe you do, too?

November 10

> "With man this is impossible, but not with God; all things are possible with God."
> Mark 10:27

How amazing is this statement? **Nothing** is impossible for God.

Jesus made this statement in response to His disciples' question about how hard it is for a rich person to be saved. His response is wonderful, because it reminds you that none of your problems are too big for Him.

You can be sure that He can handle any prayer request you have. Never give up on God – He can do anything!

LIVING IT

Kendall used to pray a lot. He faithfully lifted up his friends and family in prayer. But now he has something to pray about that is really big. It's so big that he isn't sure even God can handle it. His grandpa is really sick and he might even die. Kendall loves his grandpa a lot. He knows he should pray for him, but he isn't sure God can make him well.

Actually the truth is that he wasn't sure until he read this verse. Now he knows he can pray for Grandpa and anything else, because nothing is impossible with God!

November 11

GIVE ALL TO JESUS

Jesus wants 100% of you. The guy who surrenders completely to Him will never be sorry. Jesus promises that!

When He says you will get back 100 times what you give Him, is He talking about money? No. Money doesn't matter to Jesus.

He's talking about the blessings of knowing and serving Him – peace, joy, assurance that you are loved, purpose in your life, prayers heard and the promise of eternal life. Blessings too great to even count.

"I tell you the truth," Jesus replied, "no one who has left home or brothers or sisters or mother or father or children or fields for Me and the gospel will fail to receive a hundred times as much in this present age and in the age to come, eternal life."
Mark 10:29-30

LIVING IT

Avery doesn't get what Jesus means about leaving your family and your work to follow Jesus. He wonders if He is saying that the only people who will be blessed are those who go to other countries as missionaries.

That's not it. Jesus is just saying that nothing should be more important to Avery than serving Him. In order for that to happen, Avery has to trust Jesus enough to give up control of his life and believe that He will take complete care of him.

> "Heaven and earth will pass away, but My words will never pass away."
>
> Mark 13:31

God's Word is a gift to you. The Bible is God's message to you. It contains much of what He wants you to know about Him and His care for you. He is pleased when you read it because you get to know Him better through it.

God's Word has survived through the centuries even though people have tried to destroy it. Jesus says that it will never be lost. No matter what else happens, God's Word will survive for you.

LIVING IT

Reading God's Word is like having a conversation with God. The more you read God's Word the better you get to know Him and the more you understand about Him.

You like to talk with your friends, don't you? Talking with your friends is how you find out what they believe and what is important to them. Well, that's what you learn about God by reading His Word. Take time to read it – He wrote it for you!

WORSHIP MATTERS

Think about this woman. She was a nobody in the eyes of the men who were around Jesus that day.

Women weren't considered very important at that time. But, this woman worshiped Jesus by pouring expensive perfume on Him. The men there criticized her for that. But, Jesus knew she was worshiping Him.

What she did was so important that it was recorded in the Bible and people are still talking about her thousands of years later. Worship matters.

LIVING IT

Worship happens in different ways for different people. Phil worships through music – singing it and listening to it. Larry worships through words – reading and writing. Travis worships through art – painting and observing. Worship is a very personal experience and comes from a heart surrendered to God and focused on honoring and praising Him.

HE'S COMING BACK

> "I am," said Jesus. "And you will see the Son of Man sitting at the right hand of the Mighty One and coming on the clouds of heaven."
>
> Mark 14:62

A religious leader point-blank asked Jesus if He was the Messiah. Jesus' answer was, "I am."

Jesus knew that the man asking Him the question was not a friend, but He pointedly answered that He is indeed God's Son, the Messiah.

And not only that, He promised that He would one day come back to earth to judge the sins of mankind.

LIVING IT

Often when Jesus talked about coming back to take His followers to heaven, He was speaking to His friends and His words were filled with hope and promise.

This time, He seems to speak more firmly and the idea of judgment comes through. Perhaps He was trying to get His listeners to take Him seriously and get their lives in order by obeying and serving Him. He will come back. Be ready.

ONE WAY

The pathway to salvation and being with Jesus forever in heaven is a personal one. Each person must make his own choice about believing.

You can't count on salvation just because your parents or friends are saved. There is only one way to salvation – believe. The person who does not believe is not saved and will not go to heaven.

LIVING IT

Accepting Jesus as Savior is a big decision to Ken. It isn't one he will make lightly. Right now he doesn't see the necessity of it. His mom and dad are strong Christians so he's pretty sure he will get to heaven with them. After all, they take him everywhere now.

Well, not this time Ken. He must make his own personal decision to believe in Jesus and accept Him as Savior. That's the only way!

> "It is written: 'Man does not live on bread alone.'"
> Luke 4:4

Satan tempted Jesus to try to get Him to turn away from God and honor Satan. Jesus didn't do it, of course. But you learn some interesting things during this experience.

One is to stop thinking about yourself, whether you're hungry, cold, poor, rich, or whatever. Jesus didn't think about His needs when He was being tempted. He focused on God and He depended on Scripture to get Him through the temptation.

Don't focus on your physical needs, instead, focus on Jesus and His care for you.

LIVING IT

Robert's dad lost his job and the whole family has had to cut corners just to make ends meet. In fact, sometimes Robert is hungry when he goes to bed because there just isn't enough food. Truthfully, it's hard to think about anything else when he is hungry.

Robert could focus all his energy on that, but this verse tells him not to do that. Even when he's hungry he can remember that God is the most important and He will take care of everything.

November 17

HUMBLE HEARTS

"Blessed are you who are poor, for yours is the kingdom of God."

Luke 6:20

This doesn't mean you have to be financially poor to be a part of God's kingdom. You just need to be humble and dependent on God.

That is sometimes a difficult thing for wealthy and powerful people. They may be used to being in charge rather than surrendered to someone else's will.

Jesus lived an example of this humility – serving others, helping people who others ignored and by doing what God wanted Him to do.

LIVING IT

The cool thing about Tim is that he has a lot to be proud of. He's an excellent student and a star athlete. He even is a great musician. He could be filled with pride, but he isn't.

Tim is one of the nicest, most humble guys ever. He cares about other people and he really encourages others to do well. He never brags about himself or his successes. Tim serves God by serving and loving others.

November 18

WHAT WE REALLY NEED

> "Blessed are you who hunger now, for you will be satisfied."
>
> Luke 6:21

What do you hunger for? What do you want more and more and more of? Time with friends? Popularity? Game time in a sport? Knowledge? Knowing God better? Jesus said that if you hunger for the right things you will be satisfied. Hunger for a desire to know God better, serve Him more fully, be more obedient to Him. That's what will make you feel satisfied and fulfilled.

LIVING IT

When Reed asked Jesus into his heart he knew that he loved Jesus. He has been reading his Bible and getting to know Jesus better and that has helped him love Jesus more.

Reed doesn't understand everything he reads in God's Word, but he asks his parents or Sunday school teacher to explain things. The more he reads, the more he **wants** to read. Reed can't get enough of learning about Jesus and His amazing love for him!

November 19

BLESSED OBEDIENCE

"Blessed are you when men hate you, when they exclude you and insult you and reject your name as evil because of the Son of Man."

Luke 6:22

Some people will not like you simply because you follow Jesus. Your obedience to God will make them uncomfortable and they may show that by making fun of you, shutting you out of their groups of friends and just generally insulting you.

Jesus reminds you that it's OK. He will bless you for your obedience to Him!

LIVING IT

Nick is running for class president. His opponent, Donnie, does not fight fair. He knows that Nick is a Christian and tries to live his life in obedience to God. So Donnie starts a "whisper campaign" about that. A whisper campaign is when he drops little comments to others about Nick being a religious freak. Donnie says things like Nick is no fun because his head is always in the Bible, things like that. Their classmates start wondering if Nick can be a good president. Nick is being insulted just because he follows God. God will bless Nick for his obedience.

November 20

SERVE GOD OR MONEY

"Woe to you who are rich, for you have already received your comfort."
Luke 6:24

Money. Some people never have enough. The more they have, the more they want. Sure, they share some of their money. The sad thing is that all their focus is on getting more money and then on investing their money and protecting their money. Life becomes all about money. It's sad because this person doesn't make serving, loving and obeying God his focus, but thinks more about money than God. Well, the money is all he's going to have in the long run, not God.

LIVING IT

Roy has a great example of the opposite of this statement. His mom and dad both work hard at their jobs and they earn enough money to make life comfortable for the family. But, money isn't their goal. They make sure there is time to spend together as a family and they spend time with other families and friends. They generously give money to help others and they spend time helping others. Roy sometimes goes with them to work in the food pantry and other things they do. Their focus is on serving God, not money.

THINKING OF OTHERS

> "Woe to you who are well fed now, for you will go hungry. Woe to you who laugh now, for you will mourn and weep."
>
> Luke 6:25

So, is Jesus saying that it is better for you to be hungry and sad? No, He isn't saying that. But, Jesus hopes you will notice when others do not have enough food or need help, and be willing to do the helping.

If a guy thinks only about himself and his needs or about having fun, then woe to him. But, if he helps others who do not have enough of what they need, then he is being Jesus to them. No more woes.

LIVING IT

Some guys think, "I'm just a kid, what can I do to help someone who doesn't have enough food?" Some guys would think that, then forget about it and get themselves a snack, but not Thomas.

He heard that the food pantry was short on peanut butter. So, he started collecting jars of peanut butter. He made flyers and put it up around town. He went door to door collecting it. Then, when he had jars and jars of peanut butter to donate, he had a Donate-the-Peanut-Butter-Party doing it!

> "A student is not above his teacher, but everyone who is fully trained will be like his teacher."
>
> Luke 6:40

Some guys are hard to teach because they think they know everything already. When the teacher tries to explain a lesson, these guys won't listen. After all, they know the answers better than the teacher.

Yeah, right. Jesus reminds you that you do not know more than He does. Only by having an open mind and heart, can you learn to be like Jesus.

LIVING IT

William takes drum lessons. He enjoys playing, but isn't very cooperative with his teacher. He doesn't like doing the exercises that are necessary to become a good musician. When his teacher assigns exercises, William argues that he doesn't need to do them. This is a classic example of the student thinking he knows more than his teacher. He will only learn to be a better drummer if he accepts training from his teacher. In the same way, you will only learn to be a better Christian by accepting training from Jesus. Understand that you do not know more than your teacher, and have an open spirit to learn from Him.

GOOD FROM GOOD

> "Each tree is recognized by its own fruit. People do not pick figs from thornbushes, or grapes from briers."
>
> Luke 6:44

It's hopeless to expect good to come from bad. If you try to make a fancy dinner using weeds and dirt, you'll be disappointed.

If you expect good and kind behavior from a heart that cares nothing about God or others, you will also be disappointed. Jesus' example of a tree having fruit of a certain kind shows that He knows a heart that is devoted to Him will show love and kindness to others.

A heart that doesn't know God cannot be expected to show love and concern for others.

LIVING IT

Stop thinking you can fool God. You can say all the "Christian" words. You can pray fancy prayers aloud. You can go to church every time the doors are open. You can fool all the people around you, but you will not fool God.

He sees your heart and that is where the fruit of your life comes from. Even if you do amazing, kind deeds, if your heart doesn't belong to Jesus, you are not doing it for Him.

November 24

THE FIRMEST FOUNDATION

"I will show you what he is like who comes to Me and hears My words and puts them into practice. He is like a man building a house, who dug down deep and laid the foundation on rock. When a flood came, the torrent struck that house but could not shake it, because it was well built."

Luke 6:47-48

Sometimes people are willing to do the work of getting through problems by their trust in and knowledge of Jesus.

Jesus compares this to the example of a house built on a good foundation. Even the worst storm cannot shake it because its foundation is firm.

How does a guy build a firm foundation for life? By spending time reading God's Word, praying and building a strong relationship of trust with Jesus. Then, whatever happens in your life, your foundation will be firm.

LIVING IT

Quinton doesn't spend time with God every day. Once in a while he reads his Bible for a few minutes and he prays when there is something he wants. Maybe Quinton doesn't think this is a big deal, but the truth is that he is not building the good foundation for a strong relationship with Jesus.

When the time comes when he will need that foundation to hold him up during tough times he will crumble. But, there's still time to fix it – spend time with Jesus every day!

November 25

NO HOPELESSNESS

> "Your faith has saved you;
> go in peace."
> Luke 7:50

The woman Jesus spoke these words to could have been hopeless. She had two strikes against her – she was known to live a sinful life and she was a woman.

Still, she courageously came to Jesus when He was surrounded by a group of men and she worshiped Him. Jesus probably knew her reputation of living a sinful lifestyle, but He could also see her heart. He saw that she had faith in Him. That faith saved her and promised a life of peace.

LIVING IT

Sometimes Ron feels a little hopeless. That hopelessness comes when he stops trusting Jesus and starts thinking about problems or fears he has.

Staying close to Jesus and keeping his faith and trust in Him strong is what gives Ron hope and peace. Jesus has never let him down and Ron is pretty sure that He won't start that right now!

November 26

NECESSARY FAITH

"The knowledge of the secrets of the kingdom of God has been given to you, but to others I speak in parables, so that, 'though seeing, they may not see; though hearing, they may not understand.'"

Luke 8:10

Over and over again Jesus stresses how important faith is. If you don't believe Jesus is God's Son and that He came to earth to teach about the best way to know God and that He was killed and rose back to life, then the true message of His teaching will make no sense to you. It will be like hearing someone speak a language you don't understand.

Jesus' message is for His followers.

LIVING IT

Mason and his family visited Norway. He learned a few Norwegian words and phrases before the trip, but not enough to have a conversation with anyone. So, when someone spoke to him, all he could do was nod his head and smile. He didn't understand a word. That's how the messages of Scripture sound to people who don't believe in Jesus. They can understand the basic message (which hopefully leads them to salvation), but the deeper lessons – the ones that would help them grow mature in their faith – make no sense to them. Start with the basics, then grow.

LIGHT IN DARKNESS

"No one lights a lamp and hides it in a jar or puts it under a bed. Instead, he puts it on a stand, so that those who come in can see the light."

Luke 8:16

What good is a light that is hidden? The purpose of light is to break through darkness and reveal what is hidden by that darkness.

Jesus called Himself the Light of the World and when a guy asks Jesus to be his Savior, His light comes into the guy's life. He becomes one more point of light for Jesus in a world filled with the darkness of sin.

LIVING IT

Drew is the first person in his whole family to become a Christian. It's kind of scary, but he is able to be a light for Jesus to his family. How does he do that?

Drew does it by showing patience, love, unselfishness and by being concerned about his family members, and just generally showing love. Drew gives the credit for all this kindness to Jesus, because it is by His power that he has changed from how he once behaved.

November 2

> "There is nothing hidden that will not be disclosed, and nothing concealed that will not be known or brought out into the open."
>
> Luke 8:17

Secrets are fun sometimes. But, secrets that you are trying to keep someone from knowing, maybe about something wrong you've done are not good.

Here's an interesting thing about secrets – you can't keep them from God. He knows and sees everything. Everything will be revealed to Him eventually and you will have to answer to Him for the choices you have made.

LIVING IT

Charlie thinks he is pretty sneaky and pretty smart. He has the idea that the things he thinks, but doesn't say out loud and the things he reads or watches on the computer when he is alone are secrets and that no one knows about them.

He's so wrong. Jesus knows Charlie's thoughts and He sees his actions. One day Charlie will answer to Him for those things. There are no secrets from God.

November 29

GOOD LISTENING

> "Therefore consider carefully how you listen. Whoever has will be given more; whoever does not have, even what he thinks he has will be taken from him."
>
> Luke 8:18

What kind of listener are you? Do you hear the first couple of words someone says to you then shut your ears, because you think you know what the rest of the sentence is? Do you listen with your mind already made up?

Listening with an open mind and heart is the best way to learn new things. If you listen with your mind made up already, thinking that you know everything, you will not learn very much.

LIVING IT

Sean is annoying to talk with, because he can't wait for someone to finish a sentence. He always finishes it himself. Sean's friends have pretty much stopped talking with him, because he doesn't listen anyway.

Sean does the same thing with God. He thinks he has all the answers so there's no reason to listen to teaching from His Word or to be quiet before Him and listen for His voice of guidance. Sean is not learning more about God by behaving this way. He must listen to God and have a heart that is open to learn.

November 30

DECEMBER

"Whoever welcomes this little child in My name welcomes Me; and whoever welcomes Me welcomes the One who sent Me. For he who is least among you all – he is the greatest."

Luke 9:48

People who think they are important or powerful often associate only with other important or powerful people. They think they are too important to have anything to do with those who are not as important as they are.

These people really miss the point of Jesus' teaching. Power and importance mean nothing to Him.

Humility, love for others, devotion to Jesus – those are some of the things that make you great.

LIVING IT

What does this teaching mean to someone your age? Think about it. Are you friendly to those who aren't as popular as you are? Are you kind to those who aren't kind to you? Do you take time to talk with younger guys and be an example to them of a kind, loving Christian guy?

Jesus consistently makes a point that kindness and concern for others is most important in living for Him.

December 1

BE STILL

It's good to be busy. Martha was super busy preparing dinner. But she was not only busy, she was annoyed that her sister wasn't helping her.

Mary was just sitting beside Jesus and listening to what He said. Martha thought that Jesus should make Mary help her, but Jesus was happy that Mary wanted to spend time with Him.

That's the most important thing. Spend time with Jesus and get to know Him.

"Martha, Martha," the Lord answered, "you are worried and upset about many things, but only one thing is needed. Mary has chosen what is better, and it will not be taken away from her."

Luke 10:41-42

LIVING IT

David is a "take-charge" guy, a real leader. If you want something done, put David in charge and you can be sure that it will be taken care of.

However, the struggle David has is to keep balance in his life between being busy, but also being quiet with Jesus. Really being quiet. That means not talking, reading, watching TV or anything, just being quiet to hear what Jesus wants to say to him. It's not easy, especially for a busy guy like David. But it is important.

December 2

"So I say to you: Ask and it will be given to you; seek and you will find; knock and the door will be opened to you."

Luke 11:9

Jesus had just taught His followers the prayer that is known as the Lord's Prayer. He follows that up with this statement, which is a promise that God hears your prayers.

He loves you and wants to give you good gifts. But, don't consider God a big "Santa Claus" who will give you absolutely anything you want. It doesn't work that way.

Ask, seek and knock as you spend time in His Word and praying. Then your requests will be guided by His Spirit.

LIVING IT

Prayer is an amazing privilege. Seriously. Think about it. You have the listening ear of the Creator of all things, the most powerful being in the universe. What are you going to do with that opportunity?

He tells you to ask, seek and knock. Do you believe that He will answer? Do you trust His answers? Pray with confidence and trust the results.

December 3

JUST ASK

Way back in the Old Testament the Holy Spirit was promised to God's people one day.

The Spirit is an amazing gift to people. He lives in your heart so that God's guidance is always with you.

Jesus obviously considers the Holy Spirit to be a very special gift and one that is given because of true love by God for His children.

> "If you then, though you are evil, know how to give good gifts to your children, how much more will your Father in heaven give the Holy Spirit to those who ask Him!"
> Luke 11:13

LIVING IT

Just ask for the Spirit. Does it seem strange to you that you have to ask for the Holy Spirit? Well, since you have to ask then you must think about it and having the Spirit in your life becomes your choice. It has to be something you really want. That way you won't take it lightly. The gift of the Spirit is evidence of the true love the Father has for you. He wants to give you wonderful, amazing things because He loves you so much. The Spirit is the best of all gifts. Receive Him seriously and call on Him daily for guidance and understanding.

December 4

> "Blessed rather are those who hear the word of God and obey it."
>
> Luke 11:28

A woman in the crowd had just called out, "Blessed is Your mother who gave You birth!" and Jesus' response is this verse. Not only hearing God's Word is important, but obeying it is what gives blessings. Jesus wasn't dismissing His earthly mother as unimportant, but was emphasizing how very important it is to hear and obey God's Word.

LIVING IT

Eli has heard God's Word his whole life. His family has devotions together every night. His parents take all the kids to church and Sunday school. So, Eli has heard all the Bible stories and memorized all the verses to get his club badges.

But just hearing the Word doesn't do him much good. It's when Eli understands the Word of God and obeys it that he begins understanding it and is blessed. He is living for Jesus when he obeys God's Word.

December 5

GIVE TO THE POOR

This is the end of a story Jesus told about a rich man who had so many crops that he didn't know what to do. Instead of sharing what he had with those who didn't have enough food, he just built a bigger barn to store all he had.

He thought he was set for life. But, his life would end that very night and he would learn that he had not pleased God by thinking only of himself instead of how he could help others.

"God said to him, 'You fool! This very night your life will be demanded from you. Then who will get what you have prepared for yourself?' This is how it will be with anyone who stores up things for himself but is not rich toward God."
Luke 12:20-21

LIVING IT

Over and over Jesus said not to worry about money. He said not to try to get more and more money. He said to use just what you need, then give to the poor. He said to care about others more than you care about yourself. Chase gets it because his parents have set a good example. His parents are generous to organizations that help the poor. They've taught Chase to share a part of his allowance, too. They give not only of their money, but their time as well to help in any way they can. They are storing up treasures in heaven.

TRUSTING GOD

> "Therefore I tell you, do not worry about your life, what you will eat; or about your body, what you will wear. Life is more than food, and the body more than clothes."
>
> Luke 12:22-23

Worry may be the biggest enemy for a Christian. It's hard not to worry, but the truth is that worry and trust cannot live in your heart at the same time.

If you trust God to take care of you and give you what you need, then you will not be worried about those things. If you don't trust Him, well, that's where worry comes in.

You must learn that you can always trust God to take care of you.

LIVING IT

Jason's family is moving across the country. He has to leave his friends, grandparents, school, church and home behind. Everything will be new and Jason is kind of scared. OK, he's not worried about food, but he does kind of wonder what his new school will be like. He's worried that he won't be able to make friends. The truth is that he's worried about being lonely.

If Jason would only trust God with these things and tell Him what he's afraid of and let God take care of those worries, then he wouldn't be so worried. It's not easy, but when he does it he will be so glad he did!

WORLD-CLASS WORRY

"Who of you by worrying can add a single hour to his life? Since you cannot do this very little thing, why do you worry about the rest?"

Luke 12:25-26

You can worry nonstop about how long you're going to live, but you can't do anything about it. You can't do a thing to change it. So, why worry?

Jesus wants you to know that you can trust Him with absolutely everything. He loves you more than you can imagine so why not trust Him to take complete care of you, every moment of every day that He gives you in this life?

LIVING IT

Peyton is a world-class worrier. Yeah, he is really good at it. He worries about earthquakes and storms. He worries that his friends will get mad at him. He worries that his dad will lose his job. Peyton even worries that he will get sick. Seriously, he worries about everything.

As is true with most worriers, Peyton mostly worries about things that he can't do anything about. Peyton will learn to trust Jesus to take care of everything.

December 8

"Where your treasure is, there your heart will be also."
Luke 12:34

Some people try to divide their heart. They think it's possible to put all their energy, thoughts and time into one thing, but then say that their heart belongs totally to God. It doesn't work.

The reality is that your treasure becomes whatever occupies your time, thoughts and energy and if it isn't knowing and serving God, then your treasure is in the wrong place.

LIVING IT

December 9

Carl has a real gift for playing the saxophone. He practices hours on end to improve his playing. He listens to recordings of great saxophonists when he isn't practicing. Carl's life and thoughts are consumed with improving his playing ability. The thing is that Carl would also say that his heart is devoted to God. It's fine that he is a good saxophone player who wants to improve his skill – after all, God gave him the gift. The problem comes in when anything occupies your time and thoughts so much that you don't make time to spend time with God or care about others, then your treasure is in the wrong place.

PRIDE COMES BEFORE A FALL

> "Everyone who exalts himself will be humbled, and he who humbles himself will be exalted."
>
> Luke 14:11

Do you think you are someone special? Someone who is better than those around you? Do you need to be Number One, center of attention, life of the party? Well then, you are probably going to take a tumble.

Jesus said it. If you're filled with pride in yourself, you're going to get a reality check. The people you are pushing down as you push yourself up, well, they may end up more important than you!

LIVING IT

Christopher wants to be "a somebody" and he will do pretty much anything to make sure that happens. He has even resorted to telling lies about other guys so that their friends will like him more. He makes fun of those he considers weaker. He bullies younger guys. What's going to happen? The guys will figure out how selfish Christopher is and eventually he won't be popular at all. The people he has been lying about will end up having more friends than he does. It's the same lesson Jesus always teaches – think about how you treat others. Be kind. Be friendly.

"When you give a banquet, invite the poor, the crippled, the lame, the blind, and you will be blessed. Although they cannot repay you, you will be repaid at the resurrection of the righteous."

Luke 14:13-14

Once again Jesus makes the point that the guy who follows Him does not pay attention only to those who are popular, powerful, wealthy, healthy or useful to him.

Pay attention to the people the world pushes aside. Help them. Be their friends. No, they can't pay you back for your kindness, but Jesus will pay you back one day. Count on it.

LIVING IT

Vince's birthday is coming up. He's planning a fantastic party. Now, he could just invite his closest friends to this fancy party or he could have a simpler party and invite everyone in his class, including the kids who never get invited to parties – the kids who don't really have any friends.

Yeah, that's what Vince will do. Pay attention to those who don't receive much attention. It's the Jesus way.

December 11

PARTY ON!

> "I tell you that in the same way there will be more rejoicing in heaven over one sinner who repents than over ninety-nine righteous persons who do not need to repent."
>
> Luke 15:7

Think about it. The moment you accepted Christ as your Savior a party broke out in heaven! A party because of you! That's how much Jesus loves you.

Every time a person accepts Jesus there is a party in heaven. He doesn't love one person more than another, but Jesus' desire is that all people would accept Him. He wants all people to be a part of His family.

LIVING IT

So what? If you've accepted Jesus then your party has already happened, right? So why does this verse matter to you?

Two reasons. Firstly, stop and enjoy the thought that the angels and all the residents of heaven rejoiced because you joined the family. Second, you have a role to play now in helping others find Jesus. You can have a part in someone else's party!

December 12

CELEBRATION

> "'My son,' the father said, 'you are always with me, and everything I have is yours. But we had to celebrate and be glad, because this brother of yours was dead and is alive again; he was lost and is found.'"
>
> Luke 15:31-32

Grace is when you get something you don't deserve. That's what the young boy called the Prodigal Son received – grace.

And, when this boy who had wasted his father's money and hurt his father so badly came home, his father threw a party. The older son, who had always been home, wasn't happy about this party.

He wasn't able to be happy that his brother had come home. He couldn't rejoice with his father. He was too selfish.

LIVING IT

Where do you fit in this story? Would you be like the Prodigal Son who hurt his dad by leaving home and wasting all his money and who had to come back and ask his dad for a job? Would you be like the older brother who said, "Hey, what about me?"

Do you see that God celebrates when anyone comes to Him? When a child who has wandered away comes back, that is even more reason to celebrate! It is the grace of God giving forgiveness and acceptance even when it isn't deserved.

December 13

GOOD PRIORITIES

"No servant can serve two masters. Either he will hate the one and love the other, or he will be devoted to the one and despise the other. You cannot serve both God and money."

Luke 16:13

There seems to be two main points that Jesus emphasizes over and over in His teachings. Those two points are: Don't put a lot of importance on money and think about others before yourself.

The thing with money is either you have it or you don't. And, if you don't, then you want some. If you do, then you want more.

Money is OK, but it should be shared with those who don't have enough and getting it and keeping it should never be more important than serving God and loving others.

LIVING IT

Dallas doesn't have money. He doesn't have a job. He's just a kid, so the message of not serving two masters (God and money) doesn't seem to really apply to him. But, it does, because right now he is developing what his priorities will be as he grows up. Dallas tries to keep his focus on putting the most value on his relationship with God and not letting money or success be too important to him.

He is also careful to give some of whatever money he has back to God's work to help others. Good priorities.

> "Were not all ten cleansed? Where are the other nine?"
> Luke 17:17

Ten men who had leprosy called out to Jesus. Ten men asked Him to heal them. Ten men believed that He could.

Jesus healed all ten and sent them to town to show the priests that they had been healed.

One man came back to say thank you.

Nine did not. Only one man praised God for the miracle of healing.

Saying thank you is important. When Jesus does something for you, thank Him.

LIVING IT

Terry has learned this lesson well. His parents taught him to say thanks to people who did something for him. They taught him to write thank you notes for gifts. They taught him to make thankfulness a major part of his prayer life.

Terry tries to never take God's blessings for granted. He tries to remember to always say thank you for everything God gives him and does for him.

HEART KINGDOM

"The kingdom of God does not come with your careful observation, nor will people say, 'Here it is' or 'There it is,' because the kingdom of God is within you."

Luke 17:20-21

The kingdom of God is not something you have to look for way in the future. Yes, there will be a day when Jesus will come to get His followers and take them to heaven. But, the kingdom of God is also right here and now.

Because Jesus died for your sins, rose back to life and now lives in your heart, and because the Holy Spirit was given to you, the kingdom of God is right now – in you!

LIVING IT

Nate is a new person. A brand-new person. Oh sure, he has the same skin, hair and teeth. It would be weird if that was new, wouldn't it? But, on the inside Nate is new. He asked Jesus to come into his heart and be his Savior and immediately he knew that something was different in his heart. As he lets Jesus take control of his thoughts and actions, he sees that he is becoming kinder. He is more concerned for other people. Nate has much more love for those around him. Nate's family has noticed it, too. God's kingdom is now in Nate's heart!

December 16

"Let the little children come to Me, and do not hinder them, for the kingdom of God belongs to such as these. I tell you the truth, anyone who will not receive the kingdom of God like a little child will never enter it."

Luke 18:16-17

Once again Jesus points out that the strong and powerful people in the world are not really so important as they may think.

It's important to receive God's kingdom like a child – with humility, trust and dependence on Jesus. That's the only way to enter God's kingdom, because pride and power won't get you in.

LIVING IT

John thinks this verse is so cool because even grown-ups need to come to Jesus like a child. Why does he think it is cool? Because it puts everyone on the same level.

No one is more important to Jesus or in His kingdom than anyone else is. Everyone bows down to Jesus and worships Him with faith, hope and love. That's the way it should be. He is in control and everyone bows to Him.

December 17/

A RICH MAN

> "You still lack one thing. Sell everything you have and give to the poor, and you will have treasure in heaven. Then come, follow Me."
>
> Luke 18:22

A rich man came to Jesus and asked how to get eternal life. Jesus mentioned some commandments and the man said, "Yes, I've obeyed those."

But there was one more thing Jesus wanted the man to do. He wanted the man to get rid of everything he owned – everything he had worked so very hard to get. Sell it all and not even keep the money but give it to the poor.

Once again, Jesus makes the point that it is important to take care of others. If they don't have bread and you do, share it with them!

LIVING IT

When Bill read the story of the rich man and what Jesus told him to do, it stuck in his heart. He couldn't stop thinking about it. So, Bill went to his parents with an idea. "I've got tons more toys than I can ever play with. Some I never use.

Would it be OK if I box up a bunch of my toys and donate them to kids who don't have any?" His parents thought that it was a good idea. Bill didn't donate junky, worn-out toys. He sent good ones, some that were brand new and yes, even some that he liked. Wow, he felt so good!

> "I tell you the truth," He said, "this poor widow has put in more than all the others. All these people gave their gifts out of their wealth; but she out of her poverty put in all she had to live on."
>
> Luke 21:3-4

Jesus is so observant. He saw that while the rich man in the temple put a generous gift in the offering, he actually gave just a little bit of the massive amount of money he had. He gave money that was left over after he used what he needed.

But, a poor widow who was also in the temple put two small coins in the offering. She gave more than the rich man because she gave all she had. She held nothing back from God.

LIVING IT

What's the lesson from this story? Giving to God's work is a good thing to do. Giving to poor people is a good thing to do. But, if you give only out of your extra money, that doesn't really put a strain on you, does it?

If you give all you have or even give money that you may need in order to eat yourself, it shows that you are completely surrendered to God and that you trust Him completely to take care of you.

December 19

LIVING WATER

> "If you knew the gift of God and who it is that asks you for a drink, you would have asked Him and He would have given you living water."
>
> John 4:10

You've probably heard the story of the Samaritan woman who met Jesus at a well. He asked for a drink of water and she responded rather rudely, because usually Jews wouldn't have anything to do with Samaritans.

The woman didn't understand who Jesus was. He told her that He could give her living water – water that never runs out because it is the life and joy of knowing Him.

LIVING IT

What do you think the term "living water" means? Water is necessary for life. All kinds of life from the smallest plant to human beings need water to survive. In fact, you can survive longer without food than you can without water.

Jesus is called the Water of Life, because when you ask Him into your heart, you are given a new life that will be for eternity. The water necessary for the body to survive comes from outside. The water necessary for your spirit to survive comes from Jesus.

> "Thus the saying, 'One sows and another reaps' is true. I sent you to reap what you have not worked for. Others have done the hard work, and you have reaped the benefits of their labor."
>
> John 4:37-38

The work of God in this world is done through teamwork. You are a part of His team. That's pretty cool, isn't it? It's cool because not every person has the same gift or talent.

Some people are really good at explaining the pathway to salvation, some are good at just being friends with people and showing them Jesus' love, some are good counselors, and some are good teachers.

It takes everyone playing a part for one person to come to Jesus. Everyone is necessary!

LIVING IT

Jay knows he should be able to share his faith with friends who do not know Jesus. But, he gets tongue-tied when he tries. Jay is really good at just being friends with people and showing them Jesus' love through his own actions.

Jay is an important part of God's plan to share His love with those who don't know Him. Jay can be a friend and then God will send someone else to explain salvation. It takes a team!

December 21

SPIRITUAL FOOD

> "I am the bread of life. He who comes to Me will never go hungry, and he who believes in Me will never be thirsty."
>
> John 6:35

So, is Jesus saying that people who come to Him never have to eat or drink again?

No, He isn't talking about the physical bread and water that your body needs to survive. He is talking about the nourishment your soul needs to grow stronger in Him and to trust Him more and more. He is the food and water that will feed your spirit and give you eternal life.

LIVING IT

Jon doesn't quite get what it means that Jesus is bread. It is kind of hard to understand what Jesus means. He doesn't understand how his spirit needs to be fed. But as Jon thinks back to other verses that say whatever you put inside your heart and mind is what comes out of your mouth and actions, then it makes more sense. If Jesus is his bread and water then the food he is feeding his heart is healthy and obedient to Jesus. That means Jon's actions and words will be filled with His love! Jon's faith will grow stronger and his spirit will be healthy!

> "I tell you the truth, everyone who sins is a slave to sin."
>
> John 8:34

Can you eat just one potato chip? Or one piece of chocolate? Or one of whatever is your weakness? It's hard isn't it, to stop with just one taste?

Sin is kind of like that. Once you start doing one little sin a few times, it becomes a habit that you do more often. Then, after a while, that one sin isn't enough and you begin to do more sins. Sin is addictive so that you just can't get enough of whatever is your weakness. You become a slave to sin.

LIVING IT

Rob is a slave to one particular sin – lying. He cannot stop lying. He knows with each lie that he tells that he is digging a bigger pit to get out of, but he just can't help it. Rob lies to his friends, lies about his friends, lies to his parents and even tries lying to God. He is addicted to lying, because he can't admit his mistakes and always wants to make himself look good.

The only way out of this circle of lying is to confess it to Jesus, repent and ask Jesus to give him the strength to stop.

December 23

THE GOOD SHEPHERD

"I am the good shepherd. The good shepherd lays down His life for the sheep."
John 10:11

What is a shepherd's job? To watch out for his sheep, to lead them to food and water and to protect them from harm.

Jesus is your good shepherd and He does these things for you. How? He is the Bread of Life and the Living Water that will feed and nourish your soul and He protects you from Satan's tricks.

Jesus laid down His life to protect you. He died for your sins and made it possible for you to personally know God and have eternal life with Him! He is the good shepherd.

LIVING IT

The part of this statement that speaks to Jess is that Jesus protects him. Jess lives in a home where things get a little rough sometimes. His dad has a bad temper and can get pretty harsh with all the kids but especially with Jess.

But, Jess has learned that when things get bad, he can call on Jesus for protection and care. Jesus loves him and comforts him no matter what is happening around him. Jesus gives Jess peace.

December 24

> "If you really knew Me, you would know My Father as well. From now on, you do know Him and have seen Him."
> John 14:7

This must have been an amazing statement for the disciples to hear. Jesus was a living, breathing human who they had traveled with. They had listened to Him teach and saw Him do amazing miracles. Now He tells them that by knowing Him they also know God! The only way they could truly know God was by knowing Jesus. That's true for you, also.

Jesus is the bridge to God and by getting to know Him, you learn to know God better.

LIVING IT

When you think about it, this is an amazing statement and reality. You can actually know the Creator of the Universe, the powerful, magnificent unchanging God. You can know Him!

The way you know Him is by learning to know Jesus. You learn to know Jesus by reading the Bible to learn His teachings and see how He lived and how He treated people around Him. You also see that He always submitted to God and did His will. He honored God in all He did. Good lesson for you, too, right?

JESUS' FRIENDS

> "You are My friends if you do what I command."
> John 15:14

Friendship is different from being a servant or even a student. Friends share news and they know what is going on in each other's lives. Friendship is more intimate than other relationships.

Jesus says you are His friend – if you obey Him. It's not hard, because He doesn't ask you to do things without giving you His help to do them. He asks you to do things that make you a better person and a better friend, a better son. He helps you be kind and loving.

By doing what Jesus commands, you come into friendship with Him.

LIVING IT

Ryan and Eric are best friends. They talk all the time and they dream and make plans for the future. They make each other laugh. They talk about their problems or things that make them sad. They know each other so well that they can finish each other's sentences. They can't imagine life without each other.

How cool would it be to have that kind of friendship with Jesus? How cool would it be to be super close friends with Jesus? You can become that close to Him by obeying His commands!

December 26

A CLOSE-KNIT FAMILY

"My prayer is not for them alone. I pray also for those who will believe in Me through their message, that all of them may be one, Father, just as You are in Me and I am in You. May they also be in Us so that the world may believe that You have sent Me."

John 17:20-21

Unity is important. All people who call Jesus their Savior are in the same family.

Jesus prayed for unity for all His followers. Jesus didn't want fighting among them, because that would take attention away from the message of His love.

He prayed that all of His followers would live in unity with one another and with Him and with God. That's the best way for unbelievers to see the truth of His love.

LIVING IT

Neil and Jay are in the same class. They go to the same Bible study and the same church. They've been good friends for a long time, but they recently had a big fight. They aren't even speaking to each other now! They both realize that their fight is a bad image on the work of Jesus.

If two Christian guys can't solve their problems and get along with each other, what does that say to people who don't even know Jesus yet? Why would they want to become a part of the family of God? So, Neil and Jay talk out their problems and, just as Jesus prayed, unity is restored.

December 27

COMPLETELY SURRENDERED

"Put your sword away! Shall I not drink the cup the Father has given Me?"

John 18:11

This statement has so much in it. Soldiers had come to arrest Jesus and one of His followers pulled out a sword to defend Him.

Jesus stopped His friend because He knew He was doing what God wanted Him to do.

He knew it was going to be hard. He would be tortured and murdered, but it was God's plan for Him and because He was surrendered to God and because He loves you, He was willing to do it.

LIVING IT

Barry reads this verse and thinks about what may have been going through Jesus' mind at that moment. He wonders if Jesus was scared or sad. Barry realizes how very much Jesus must love him if He was willing to face whatever God's will was for Him so that Barry would have the privilege of knowing God personally and the promise of eternal life.

It's amazing. Jesus was completely surrendered to God.

December 28

> **"Peace be with you."**
> John 20:26

Jesus said this often, "Peace be with you." Even in the middle of terrible circumstances, such as after His crucifixion, He came to His followers and said, "Peace be with you."

How could He expect them to have peace at a time like that? Because He wanted them to trust that He had a plan and that nothing that had happened surprised Him.

If they could trust Him with complete trust then they could have peace.

LIVING IT

Be at peace? thought Wes, *how on earth can I be at peace when the world seems to be falling apart? Everywhere I look there is some crisis or problem. No one in my family is in a good place right now. There are wars and earthquakes all around the world and who knows what else. How can I have peace?*

This is how, Wes – trust Jesus. None of the stuff that is happening is out of His knowledge. He knows everything and He will see you through each day. You can trust Him to take care of you. Have peace.

SEEING IS BELIEVING?

> "Because you have seen Me, you have believed; blessed are those who have not seen and yet have believed."
>
> John 20:29

One of Jesus' disciples, Thomas, just couldn't believe that Jesus had actually come back to life after being murdered. He needed to see Jesus for himself. When he did, then he believed.

That's good, but Jesus gave a special blessing to the thousands of others throughout history who have not actually physically seen Him or touched Him, yet believe He is alive.

LIVING IT

It's easy to believe something is real if you can see it with your eyes and touch it with your hands. Believing that Jesus is alive takes faith, because you can't physically see Him standing in front of you. You can't physically touch Him.

Faith is the basis for the Christian life. Jesus says that you are blessed for believing and that blessing will give you eternal life with Him! Open your heart to faith and be blessed!

A SHEPHERD'S WORK

> "Feed My sheep."
> John 21:17

Three times Jesus asked Peter if he truly loved Him. Three times Peter replied, "You know I love You."

Finally Jesus told Peter to feed His sheep. What does that mean? It means that Jesus wanted Peter to continue teaching the things Jesus had taught him. Jesus wanted Peter to help believers grow stronger in their faith in Him and to help do His work in the world.

Just as Jesus, the Good Shepherd, took care of His sheep, He wanted Peter to do the same.

LIVING IT

So what? Tony thought. *I'm not a shepherd. I'm not a teacher. I'm just a kid so what does "Feed My sheep" have to do with me?* Good question, Tony! Every believer has a role to play in the care of other Christians.

By praying for others, Tony is caring for them. By living out Jesus' commands, he is caring for others' needs. Tony does have a part in feeding the sheep, even if he doesn't realize it, and so do you!

December 31

ABOUT THE AUTHOR

Carolyn Larsen is an author, actress, and an experienced speaker with a God-given passion for ministering to women and children. She has spoken at conferences and retreats around the United States, Canada, and India. Carolyn has written over 40 books for children and adults. Her writing has won various awards, including the C. S. Lewis Silver Award. Carolyn lives in Glen Ellyn, Illinois, with her husband, Eric.

365 DAYS TO
KNOWING GOD FOR GUYS

ISBN 978-1-77036-149-2

Written especially for guys who want to get to know God
better, this 365-day devotional will help them to focus their
thoughts on God as they learn more about His greatness.